Cognitive Therapy

100 key points and techniques

*Michael Neenan and
Windy Dryden*

Routledge
Taylor & Francis Group

LONDON AND NEW YORK

First published 2004 by Brunner-Routledge
27 Church Road, Hove, East Sussex BN3 2FA

Simultaneously published in the USA and Canada
by Brunner-Routledge
29 West 35th Street, New York, NY 10001

Reprinted 2004 by Brunner-Routledge
27 Church Road, Hove, East Sussex BN3 2FA
270 Madison Avenue, New York, NY 10016

Reprinted 2005 and 2006 by Routledge
27 Church Road, Hove, East Sussex BN3 2FA
270 Madison Avenue, New York, NY 10016

*Routledge is an imprint of the Taylor & Francis Group,
an informa business*

© 2004 Michael Neenan and Windy Dryden

Typeset in Times by
Keystroke, Jacaranda Lodge, Wolverhampton
Printed and bound in Great Britain by
TJ International Ltd, Padstow, Cornwall
Paperback cover design Richard Massing

This publication has been produced with paper
manufactured to strict environmental standards and
with pulp derived from sustainable forests.

British Library Cataloguing in Publication Data
A catalogue record for this book is available from the British Library

Library of Congress Cataloging in Publication Data
Neenan, Michael.
    Cognitive therapy : 100 key points / Michael Neenan and Windy
Dryden.— 1st ed.
        p. cm.
Includes bibliographical references.
    ISBN 1–58391–880–9 (hardcover : alk. paper) — ISBN 1–58391–858–2
(pbk. : alk. paper)
1. Cognitive therapy. I. Dryden, Windy. II. Title.
RC489.C63N45 2004
616.89′142—dc22   2003025945

ISBN 10: 1–58391–880–9 (hbk)   ISBN 13: 978–1–58391–880–7 (hbk)
ISBN 10: 1–58391–858–2 (pbk)   ISBN 13: 978–1–58391–858–6 (pbk)

Contents

Examining and responding to NATS   **111**

Homework   **145**

Ways of identifying underlying assumptions and rules 159

Preface

Cognitive therapy (CT) was developed by Aaron T. Beck (b. 1921), an American psychiatrist, at the University of Pennsylvania in the early 1960s (J. S. Beck, 1995). CT seeks to ameliorate clients' emotional distress by helping them to identify, examine and modify the distorted and maladaptive thinking underlying their distress. Beck's approach initially focused on research into and the treatment of depression (Beck et al., 1979), but in the last two decades CT has been applied to an ever-increasing number of disorders, including anxiety and phobias (Beck et al., 1985), substance abuse (Beck et al., 1993), personality disorder (Sperry, 1999), obsessive-compulsive disorder (Salkovskis, 1999), post-traumatic stress disorder (Ehlers and Clark, 2000), psychosis (Morrison, 2001), bipolar disorder (Newman et al., 2002), and populations such as psychiatric inpatients (Wright et al., 1993), patients with chronic medical problems (White, 2001), children and adolescents (Friedberg and McClure, 2002), and older people (Laidlaw et al., 2003). CT has become the most popular and best-validated approach within the field of cognitive behaviour therapy (CBT); seventeen different approaches in this field have been listed (Mahoney and Gabriel, 1987).

In this book we will elaborate on 100 key points and techniques of cognitive therapy. Each elaboration will be of varying length. The 100 points and techniques will cover CT theory and practice, and examine misconceptions about this approach. The book is aimed primarily at

CT/ CBT trainees and other counsellors interested in this approach who need to be familiar with it as part of a general introduction to the current major psychotherapies. We hope that this will cover a wide readership.

Michael Neenan and Windy Dryden

Part 1

CT THEORY

1

It is not events *per se* which determine our feelings but the meanings that we attach to these events

'At the very heart of the CT [cognitive therapy] model is the view that the human mind is not a passive receptacle of environmental and biological influences and sensations, but rather that individuals are actively involved in constructing their reality' (Clark, 1995: 156). In order to understand a person's emotional response to a particular event it is important to discover the meaning he attaches to events in his life: his subjective construction of reality. For example, a person whose partner has left him believes he cannot be happy or cope on his own and becomes depressed; another person whose partner has departed feels relieved as he believes he has been freed from a 'stifling relationship'; a third person feels guilty as he views his bad behaviour as the reason for his partner's departure – the same event for each person, but not the same emotional reaction to it as each reaction is mediated by the person's view of the event. Therefore in order to change the way we feel about events we need to change the way we think about them.

This is not to argue that a person's emotional problems are simply created in her head but that the impact of adverse events (e.g. job loss) can be greatly exacerbated by the person's unhelpful thoughts and beliefs that interfere with her ability to cope constructively with such events (e.g. 'I shouldn't have lost my job. I'm worthless without one'). CT helps clients to develop alternative viewpoints in order to tackle their problems (e.g. 'I've lost my job, not my self-worth as this is not dependent on having a job'). Developing alternative viewpoints underscores the CT principle that there is *always* more than one way of seeing things and therefore a person chooses her viewpoint (Butler and Hope, 1996). Even in the unspeakable horrors of Auschwitz, Viktor Frankl, a famous psychiatrist, observed that 'everything can be taken from a man but one thing: the last of the human freedoms – to choose one's attitude in any given set of circumstances, to choose one's own way' (1985: 86).

2

Information processing becomes distorted when we experience emotional distress

CT is based on an information-processing model 'which posits that during psychological distress a person's thinking becomes more rigid and distorted, judgements become overgeneralized and absolute, and the person's basic beliefs about the self and the world become fixed' (Weisharr, 1996: 188). In an undisturbed frame of mind, a person is likely to check her impressions and appraisals of events in order to obtain clear and accurate information. When emotionally upset, the person will usually distort incoming information by introducing a consistently negative bias into her thinking so that it becomes rigid and overgeneralized, e.g. she becomes upset when she is not invited to a friend's party because she interprets the lack of an invitation as meaning that she is an unlikeable person. Instead of ascertaining the reasons for not being invited, or keeping an open mind about it, the person dwells on her supposed unlikeability. Common information processing errors found in emotional distress include:

- All or nothing thinking: situations are viewed in 'either/or terms', e.g. 'You're either a success or failure in life. I'm a failure.'
- Jumping to conclusions: judgements are rushed, e.g. a client says after the first session: 'Therapy isn't helping me.'
- Mind reading: discerning the thoughts of others without any accompanying evidence, e.g. 'My boss didn't smile at me this morning, so that means she is unhappy with my work.'
- Labelling: attaching labels to oneself instead of to one's behaviour, e.g. 'Because I failed my exam, this means I'm a failure.'
- Emotional reasoning: assuming that feelings are facts, e.g. 'I feel incompetent, so it must be true.'

Teaching clients how to identify and correct these errors in their thinking facilitates the return of information processing that is more evidence-based, flexible and relative (non-absolute). In the example in the opening paragraph, the person discovers that her friend had invited her but 'my mother forgot to pass on the message. If I hadn't got upset, then I wouldn't have jumped to conclusions.'

3

An emotional disorder is usually understood by examining three levels of thinking

These three levels of thinking are: negative automatic thoughts (NATS), underlying assumptions/rules and core beliefs.

- *NATS* are situation-specific and involuntarily 'pop into' a person's mind when he is experiencing emotional distress such as depression or anxiety. They appear plausible to the person and are difficult to turn off. NATS often lie outside immediate awareness but can be quickly brought to the client's attention by asking standard CT questions like: 'What was going through your mind at that moment when you got to the meeting late?' (Client's reply: 'I'm always late. I'm undisciplined, sloppy. My colleagues will look down on me.')
- *Underlying assumptions* (e.g. 'If I impress others, then I should get ahead in life') and *rules* (e.g. 'I should not let people down') guide behaviour, set standards and provide rules to follow. These assumptions and rules are often unarticulated. Underlying assumptions are usually identified by their 'if . . . then' construction, and rules are usually expressed in 'must' and 'should' statements. These assumptions and rules are the means by which individuals hope to avoid coming 'face to face' with their negative core beliefs (e.g. 'I'm incompetent'). The 'truth' of these beliefs is not questioned and, therefore, assumptions and rules serve to maintain and reinforce them. Trouble looms for the person when behaviour is not what it should be, standards are not met or rules are violated; 'trouble' is the activation of the bottom line (core belief). Beck *et al.* (1985) suggest that maladaptive assumptions often focus on three major issues: acceptance (e.g. 'I'm nothing unless I'm loved'), competence (e.g. 'I am what I accomplish') and control (e.g. 'I can't ask for help'). Assumptions and rules are cross-situational and are also known as intermediate beliefs because they lie between NATS and core beliefs (Beck, 1995).

- *Core beliefs* (also known as schemas) are the third level of thought and the deepest. Negative core beliefs are overgeneralized and unconditional (e.g. 'I'm worthless'). They are usually formed through early learning experiences and lie dormant until activated by relevant life events (e.g. the client sees himself as incompetent for not living up to his standards of being efficient, punctual and disciplined). Once activated, negative core beliefs process information in a biased way that confirms them and disconfirms contradictory information (e.g. 'So what if I'm mostly on time for meetings?'). Core beliefs can be about the self (e.g. 'I'm unlovable'), others (e.g. 'I can't trust anyone') and/or the world (e.g. 'Everything is against me').

How do these three levels interact? A person feels depressed when he fails to get 'A' grades in his exams. His dormant core belief, 'I'm a failure', is activated by his inability to live up to his rigid rule of living that he must be the best at everything he does and his mind is flooded with NATS: 'I can't show my face at college. Run away and hide. The whole college is laughing at me.' Working at the NATS level provides symptom-relief while tackling maladaptive assumptions/ rules, and negative core beliefs reduce a client's vulnerability to experiencing future episodes of emotional disturbance. The usual treatment strategy in CT is early intervention at the NATS level and then moving on to underlying assumptions/rules and core beliefs.

4

Thoughts, feelings, behaviour, physiology and environment are interconnected

CT does not propose a unidirectional model of emotional disorders whereby a negative thought or belief about an event leads to a feeling/physiological response which then produces a behaviour. Each one of these elements is capable of influencing the others in an interactive cycle. Greenberger and Padesky (1995) suggest that understanding how these five aspects of a person's life experience interact can help the client to understand her problems better. For example, a client who loses her job (environment), sees herself as worthless (thought), feels depressed (emotion), withdraws from social activity (behaviour) and complains of constant tiredness (physiology). A change in one of these elements, such as a return to being sociable, produces positive change in the other four: the client looks for another job (environment), sees herself as a person of worth (thought), her depressed mood lifts (emotion) and she starts to feel re-energized (physiology).

In CT, the usual 'way in' to start problem-solving is to help clients examine and change their maladaptive thoughts and beliefs as these have a crucial impact on the other four aspects of their life experiences. A core proposition in CT is that cognitive change is central to the human change process (Clark and Steer, 1996). Therefore, if emotional and behavioural improvement is to be achieved and adverse events are to be tackled constructively, then cognitive restructuring (i.e. thought and belief change) needs to occur. Sometimes cognitive interventions may not be initially helpful in treating severely depressed clients as they usually require a behavioural activation programme (e.g. planned daily activities) to raise their depressed mood (Beck *et al.*, 1979; Persons *et al.*, 2001). However, such behavioural activities are designed to test clients' assumptions that they will get no pleasure or sense of accomplishment from such activities; so cognitive restructuring is targeted indirectly.

5

Emotional reactions to events are viewed along a continuum

CT suggests that there is continuity between 'normal' emotional reactions to life events and exaggerated emotional reactions found in psychopathology (disturbances in thoughts, feelings and behaviours). As Weisharr and Beck explain:

> The cognitive content of syndromes (e.g. anxiety disorders, depression) have the same theme (e.g. danger or loss, respectively) as found in 'normal' experience, but cognitive distortions are extreme and, consequently, so are affect [emotion] and behaviour.
>
> (Weisharr and Beck, 1986: 65)

For example, a person looking over his life might experience sadness at the wasted opportunities but knows that new opportunities lie ahead; however, his sadness may intensify and become a prolonged depression if he sees such wasted opportunities as the *whole* story of his life. With physiological reactions (e.g. heart pounding, sweating, trembling), they would be the same for a person who believed he was about to be attacked (physical threat) as for a person who feared making mistakes in front of others (psychosocial threat).

Normal and exaggerated emotional reactions to events are characterized by what Beck *et al.* (1979) call 'mature' (flexible) and 'primitive' (absolute) thinking, respectively (e.g. a mature response to being disliked might be that 'you can't please everyone', whereas a primitive response might conclude that 'I'm thoroughly unlikeable'). Explaining to clients this continuum of emotional reactions to life events helps to remove some of the stigma from psychological distress and thereby normalize it (Weishaar, 1993). This normalizing process helps clients to see that they are not 'weirdos' or 'uniquely abnormal' for experiencing prolonged periods of emotional distress.

6

Emotional disorders have a specific cognitive content

Also known as the content-specificity hypothesis (Beck, 1976), this hypothesis proposes that emotional disorders have a specific cognitive content or theme running through them. For example, devaluation or loss in depression, danger or threat in anxiety, situationally specific danger in phobia, transgression in anger, and expansion in happiness. These themes are tied to Beck's concept of the 'personal domain', i.e. anything that the person considers important in her life. The nature of 'a person's emotional response – or emotional disturbance – depends on whether he perceives events as adding to, subtracting from, endangering, or impinging upon his domain' (Beck, 1976: 56). Some examples will help to explain this relationship:

- A person who prides herself on being a successful businesswoman becomes depressed when her company goes bust because she believes, 'My work is my life. Without my company, I'm nothing' (subtraction).
- A person becomes anxious that his sexual prowess will be ridiculed when he experiences sexual failure (endangerment).
- A person is delighted that she has been promoted as this is now another significant step in her career path (expansion).
- A person who enjoys peace and quiet in her life becomes very angry when her new next-door neighbour plays his music very loud (impingement).

A person may experience different emotions to the same event on separate occasions depending on the event's relevance to his personal domain, e.g. anxious on Monday when the train is late as he will then be late for a meeting which might undermine his personal standard of punctuality (endangerment), while on Tuesday he is angry when the train is late as it means more people will board the train at his station thereby restricting his personal space on the train (impingement). The content-specificity hypothesis was validated by empirical research in the 1980s (Weishaar, 1996).

7

Cognitive vulnerability to psychological disturbance

This refers to the 'unique vulnerabilities and sensitivities' (Weishaar and Beck, 1986) that predispose a person to psychological problems. What may precipitate psychological disturbance in one person (e.g. receiving a poor performance appraisal) is viewed with equanimity by another. The interplay between various factors such as childhood experiences, personality differences and developmental history determines which life events will trigger psychological distress in a particular individual. Beck (1987) proposed two broad personality types who would be at risk for depression or anxiety: sociotropy and autonomy:

> The sociotropic personality orientation places a high value on having close interpersonal relations, with a strong emphasis on being loved and valued by others. On the other hand, the autonomous personality orientation reflects a high investment in personal independence, achievement, and freedom of choice.
>
> (Clark and Steer, 1996: 81)

A typical sociotropic intermediate belief is 'I must be loved in order to be happy', while a typical autonomous intermediate belief is 'I must be a success in order to be worthwhile' (Beck, 1987). Anxiety can occur if, for example, there is a perceived threat to a close relationship or the danger of a career setback; if this perceived danger or threat is realized, then depression is likely to ensue. The match between a person's specific vulnerability (e.g. sees herself as worthless unless she is loved) and a significant life event that reflects this intermediate belief (e.g. she becomes depressed after her partner rejects her) is likened by Beck (1987) to a key fitting into a lock or, technically speaking, a stress–diathesis model where the stress is adverse life events (precipitating factors) and the diathesis is the cognitive vulnerability (predisposing factors).

8

Our thoughts and beliefs are both knowable and accessible

Between an external stimulus (e.g. being criticized) and an emotional response to it (e.g. anger) lie a person's thoughts about this event. Eliciting these thoughts helps the person to understand why she reacted in the way that she did to the event. Beck calls this 'tapping the internal communications' and states that clients can be trained 'to focus on their introspections [examining one's thoughts] in various situations. The person can then observe that a thought links the external stimulus with the emotional response' (1976: 27). Asking a client such questions as 'What was going through your mind at that moment?' or 'What were you thinking about in that situation?' can help to turn her attention inward rather than remain focused on the external event which she might assume 'caused' her emotional reaction. In the above example, the person is able to uncover her thoughts which contributed to her anger: 'How dare he criticize me! I've done nothing wrong. He's a bastard!'

A client might experience an emotional response without an obvious external stimulus to trigger it; in this case, the client needs to search for an internal stimulus such as an image (e.g. stammering in front of an audience) or a memory (e.g. being shouted at by a school-teacher) in order to understand why her feeling seemed to 'come out of the blue'.

In Point 3, we described three levels of cognition (automatic thoughts, assumptions/rules and core beliefs) in understanding emotional disorders. These levels usually correspond with the degree of difficulty in gaining access to them. Surface thoughts or negative automatic thoughts (NATS) are usually on the fringe of awareness, though they can be quickly brought 'centre stage' in the client's mind by asking the questions already mentioned above. Underlying assumptions/rules and core beliefs often remain unarticulated and, therefore, can be more difficult to gain access to. Linking NATS to underlying (intermediate and core) beliefs is achieved by asking the client to probe for the logical implications of each NAT (e.g. 'If it's true that you cry easily, what does that mean to you?') until important rules (e.g. 'I should always be strong') and core beliefs (e.g. 'I'm weak') are uncovered. Peeling away layers of personal meaning makes explicit what was previously implicit.

9

Acquisition of emotional disturbance

CT does not claim that dysfunctional thinking causes emotional distress; rather it forms an integral part of this distress. There are a number of factors which predispose individuals to psychological disturbance: genetic, biological, environmental, familial, physical, cultural, personality, developmental, cognitive. The interplay between these factors helps to form a person's idiosyncratic assumptions/rules and core beliefs about themselves, others and the world. These predisposing factors interact with relevant current events or stressors (precipitating factors) to trigger psychological disturbance. For example, a person who is told by his parents that he will never be as clever as his brothers spends his life trying to prove them wrong; when he fails to get into Oxbridge, unlike his brothers, and has to settle for a 'second-class' university, his core belief, 'I'm not good enough', is activated, leading to the development of depression. Therefore, to speak of cognitions causing emotional disorders is misleading. As Beck *et al.* point out:

> We consider that the primary pathology or dysfunction during a depression or an anxiety disorder is in the cognitive apparatus. However, that is quite different from the notion that cognition *causes* these syndromes – a notion that is just as illogical as an assertion that hallucinations cause schizophrenia.
>
> (Beck *et al.*, 1985: 85; emphasis in original)

The 'cognitive apparatus' would be the activation of negative core beliefs (e.g. 'I'm a failure') which filter information about the person's experience (e.g. 'I've never had any successes or will have') in a biased and distorted way, serving to reinforce and perpetuate these core beliefs and intensify the emotional distress associated with them. Cognitive deficits (e.g. poor concentration and recall) interfere with the person's reasoning (Weishaar, 1993).

10

Maintenance of emotional disturbance

Cognitive therapy 'considers *current* cognitive functioning crucial to the maintenance and persistence of psychological disturbance' (Clark, 1995: 158; emphasis in original). By staying in the here and now, the therapist helps the client to modify her current maladaptive automatic thoughts (e.g. 'I can't be happy without him'), assumptions (e.g. 'If he's abandoned me, then no one else will ever want me') and core beliefs (e.g. 'I'm unlovable') in order to ameliorate her psychological disturbance. Historical factors (e.g. parental neglect, bullied at school, severe acne during adolescence) that contributed to the person's current problem (e.g. depression, low self-esteem) cannot be modified; present factors that maintain it can be: as well as the cognitive factors already mentioned, the therapist would also address the client's social isolation, high alcohol consumption, poor diet and fitness so that she can look forward to new possibilities in her life rather than dwell on past misfortune and present unhappiness.

A historical perspective is usually included in therapy as it helps the therapist to understand how the client's present difficulties developed and the nature of her specific vulnerabilities to emotional distress. Also, the client may blame past events for her current problems (e.g. 'My parents always told me that I would be left on the shelf. It's their fault I am the way that I am'); however, the therapist would redirect her attention to the present, where she continues to subscribe to these destructive parental messages, and what steps she can take to develop helpful and compassionate self-messages.

Behaviour plays an important role in maintaining emotional distress as individuals act in ways that support their dysfunctional beliefs – you act as you think. For example, a client who sees himself as weak and unable to cope on his own acts in a 'helpless' way by trailing around after his wife expecting to be told what to do by her. Behavioural change would involve the client acting against his dysfunctional beliefs by making his own decisions and thereby learning to stand on his own feet. By changing his behaviour, the client can now see that his negative, global view of himself was incorrect.

11

The client as personal scientist

This refers to the client's assumed ability, with the help of the therapist, to test the validity of his dysfunctional thoughts and beliefs, which are viewed as hypotheses, and modify them in the light of the resulting data from various experiments. For example, a depressed client, who predicts that none of his friends will return his phone calls because they no longer care about him, makes six phone calls, three of which are returned, and grudgingly concedes that there could be benign reasons why the other three did not contact him (even if these three are no longer interested in him, it only proves that his prediction was partly true). An explicit assumption within the cognitive behavioural tradition is that human beings are scientists. As Wessler explains:

> Humans naturally want to understand themselves and their world, and cannot function properly in their world without prediction and control . . . humans are assumed to pose and test hypotheses, as do scientists, and to acquire their information by experimentation – or at least by taking an attitude of empiricism [gaining knowledge from experience] toward knowing and believing. Troubled persons are seen as poorly functioning scientists who could help themselves by testing their hypotheses more effectively and discarding ones that do not fit data in favour of ones that fit better.
>
> (Wessler, 1986: 6)

The image of therapy that the cognitive therapist wants to convey to her client is that of two scientists working together to define the latter's problem, to formulate and test hypotheses about it and find problem-solving options (Blackburn and Davidson, 1995). Beck *et al*. (1979) call this working together as two scientists 'collaborative empiricism'. Poor science can occur if the therapist wants only to *confirm* her hypotheses about the client's problems (e.g. 'It's definitely an approval issue') and the client continually discounts the data that contradict his negative beliefs (e.g. 'Successes don't count, failure does; therefore, I'm a failure'). Developing open-mindedness means that both therapist and client speak from the collected data rather than from personal opinion or prejudice.

Part 2

MISCONCEPTIONS ABOUT CT

Only articulate and intelligent clients can really benefit from CT

CT clients are, ideally, expected to provide detailed information about their problems; fill out inventories to obtain baseline measures regarding the severity of their presenting problems; detect their dysfunctional thinking and its relationship to their emotional distress; fill in forms to identify and distinguish between situations, thoughts and feelings; use reason and reality-testing to challenge dysfunctional thinking; negotiate, carry out and review homework assignments; and provide feedback on their learning and experiences of therapy. At first blush this seems like a highly intellectual endeavour that only the most intelligent and articulate clients will benefit from (in our experience, such clients can overcomplicate therapy by engaging in endless and unprofitable analysis of their thoughts and beliefs). Clients with limited intellectual and verbal abilities would surely flounder, let alone flourish, in such a rigorously demanding therapy.

However, as Beck *et al.* (1979) observe, high intelligence is not required from either the client or therapist. The important point is that the therapist adapts CT to the intellectual and verbal abilities of each client (e.g. getting rid of jargon and psychobabble and employing straightforward explanations of CT procedures and techniques) while not losing sight of teaching the key CT principle that how we think affects how we feel and behave. If some clients do find CT hard going, this is not implicit in its theory or practice that it should be so, but may be due to the lack of ingenuity on the therapist's part (e.g. keeping rigidly to 'textbook' CT).

CT has been shown to be effective with clients from different social and educational backgrounds (Persons *et al.*, 1988) and has been adapted for working with, among others, older people (Laidlaw *et al.*, 2003), learning disabilities (Kroese *et al.*, 1997), children and young people (Stallard, 2002) and adult male offenders (Altrows, 2002).

13

CT does not focus on feelings

The word 'cognitive' may give the impression that cognitive thera-pists focus only on thoughts and exclude feelings. This is untrue, as emotions are the starting point for therapeutic intervention – after all, clients usually come to therapy complaining of how they are feeling, not about what they are thinking. Thoughts and feelings are continually linked in therapy by the therapist teaching the cognitive model and the client filling in the daily thought record (DTR) forms (see Appendix 2). As Blackburn and Davidson emphasize:

> Cognitive therapy cannot progress without taking emotions into consideration *at all times*. If the patient cannot have access to his painful emotions, he and the therapist will not be able to elicit the negative thoughts which need attending to. Put simply, cognitive therapy *cannot* take place without first eliciting relevant emotional reactions.
>
> (Blackburn and Davidson, 1995: 203; emphases in original)

The first cognitive therapy treatment manual, *Cognitive Therapy of Depression* (Beck *et al.*,1979), contained a chapter called 'The role of emotions in cognitive therapy' and stressed that the therapist 'needs to be able to empathize with the patient's painful emotional experi-ences' (1979: 35). Discussing a client's problems without reference to how they feel would be a pointless cerebral exchange and would mean that Beck's 1976 book, *Cognitive Therapy and the Emotional Disorders*, had been wrongly titled and should have been called 'Cognitive Therapy and the Thinking Disorders'. Emotion needs to be activated in the sessions in order to gain access to a client's 'hot' (emotionally charged) cognitions, which will then enable cognitive restructuring (thought and belief change) to begin – e.g. a client relives a situation where she continues to feel intense guilt over a 'one night stand' with a friend of her husband's and considers herself 'thoroughly bad' for what she has done; helping the client to distinguish between the act and herself (the act does not define the whole person) reduced the intensity of her guilt.

Therapists 'should be skilled at eliciting affect [emotion] if the client does not express it spontaneously' (Dattilio and Padesky, 1990: 2). Emotional change (e.g. 'How would you like to feel instead of angry all the time?') is fundamental to the practice of CT: 'The success of CT is in part judged by reductions in negative emotional responses like sadness and fear, as well as concomitant increases in positive emotions' (Clark, 1995: 160).

14

CT is basically positive thinking

'Always look on the bright side of life because for every negative thought there is always a positive one waiting to be embraced.' This can be very difficult to hear for a client who is reeling from the effects of a traumatic event, struggling to resolve a dilemma or 'bear the unbearable' like the loss of a child. Telling a client that things 'will turn out all right for you', or 'there is always someone worse off than you', can be interpreted by the client as just another way of saying 'pull yourself together and stop making such a fuss'. CT is not based on positive thinking, but realistic thinking: 'When a patient says his life is "bad", the therapist doesn't try to convince him his life is "good". Rather, the main thrust is on *gathering accurate information to pinpoint and counteract distortions . . . in order to make adaptive decisions*' (Beck *et al.*, 1979: 299; emphasis in original).

For example, a client who claims that his professional credibility has been 'destroyed' after experiencing a panic attack in front of a large audience would not be reassured by the therapist that 'everyone still thinks well of you and your reputation is still intact'. After all, how would she know? Rather, she would encourage her client to look at the evidence for and against his belief that his credibility has been destroyed: e.g., respectively, 'Some people told me to give up public speaking if I want to avoid making a spectacle of myself again' vs. 'The feedback I get is generally just as good as it was before the panic attack'. Based on the evidence, his credibility has vanished or been diminished in some people's eyes, though certainly not everyone's, and he decides to continue with his public speaking engagements. The client is not expected to 'feel good' about the panic attack but is expected to consider the possibility of experiencing another one (e.g. 'Experts are not immune from panic attacks') and how to cope constructively with it if it does occur.

Positive thinking (e.g. 'In every way I'm getting better and better') should not be confused with developing a positive outlook (e.g. 'Whatever bad things happen in my life, I can usually find a way forward, so I'm not particularly worried about this latest setback'): the former relies on a mindless optimism untempered by unpalatable facts that may need to be faced, whereas the latter is based on assessing accurately the evidence to date. Positive affirmations (e.g. swapping 'I'm a failure' for 'I'm a great guy') are avoided as they are global and inaccurate judgements of a person; instead, particular thoughts and behaviours that are proving troublesome for the person (e.g. 'I'm worrying that I might have a serious illness even though my GP says everything is fine. I can't sleep') are focused on and tackled.

CT seems too simple

This misconception often arises because of the confusion between the meanings of 'simple' and 'simplistic': straightforward vs. too simple. CT is not simplistic; it attempts to follow the law of parsimony or Ockham's razor: 'If you can explain something adequately without introducing further complexity, then the simple explanation is the best explanation' (Warburton, 2000: 97). The cognitive therapist attempts to follow Ockham's razor by looking for simple explanations and solutions rather than complex ones (Freeman and Dattilio, 1992). For example, if a fear of spiders can be overcome in a few sessions of graded exposure to them, then detailed investigation into how this fear was acquired, how it developed, the impact it has had on the client's life, and 'Why me?' speculations will encumber and needlessly prolong a relatively straightforward treatment procedure – complexity that adds nothing of clinical significance to the treatment or outcome.

Another example: a client complains of feeling angry when her boss gives her extra work (e.g. 'It's not bloody fair! Because I finish my work first, I get punished for being efficient'). Understanding and moderating the client's anger will not be enhanced by her attempting to pinpoint her boss's motives (e.g. 'Maybe he's got problems at home and bringing them to work') or developing a psychological profile of him (e.g. 'He's an embittered middle manager, squeezed from above and below, and this is where he will be stuck, without further promotion prospects, until he retires; so he's taking it out on whoever he can'). Helping the client to see that she is not exempt from experiencing unfairness in the workplace (or anywhere else) and addressing her concerns to her boss may prove to be straightforward solutions to her anger problem.

Even when complex explanations are justified, Ockham's razor still applies, as Naugle and Follette point out:

> While we favor simple explanations, it should be noted that the law of parsimony specifies the simplest *sufficient* explanation

for a stated purpose. Thus, there is nothing inconsistent within a multifactor explanation for a set of clinical issues if they produce a better outcome than a simpler but less effective outcome.

(Naugle and Follette, 1998: 67; emphasis in original)

For example, a client may blame her current feelings (e.g. anxiety, anger, depression) and life dissatisfactions (e.g. with her job and marriage) on a car accident she was involved in several years earlier. However, on closer examination, some of her current feelings (e.g. anger) are due to current difficulties (e.g. misbehaving children, interfering in-laws), her continuing anxiety about being involved in another car accident is maintained by her avoidance of driving on her own (e.g. 'I can't trust myself on my own'), while her life dissatisfactions were present *before* the accident and have been exacerbated since (e.g. her husband has increased his infidelities and become more remote). This is a multifactor explanation that accounts sufficiently for the client's current feelings and dissatisfactions and helps her to see and act on the insight that simply blaming the car accident for all her present woes will keep her trapped and miserable instead of becoming an active problem-solver.

While CT favours simple explanations whenever possible, this does not mean that training as a cognitive therapist is a simple process: 'It takes as long to train a cognitive therapist as it does to train any therapist to practice any model of treatment effectively' (Freeman and Dattilio, 1992: 378). To an outsider, CT may seem simple to implement (deceptively simple we would argue) but, as many leading cognitive therapists repeatedly point out (e.g. Weishaar, 1996), it is not easy to do CT well.

CT is little more than symptom relief

Because CT is relatively brief, it can appear to therapists from other orientations that it only provides symptom relief for clients' problems by focusing on their here-and-now concerns and neglecting to explore underlying issues or beliefs, the apparent source of their present troubles; in other words, it is not depth-centred – the true focus of therapy. As we discussed in Point 3, a client's problems can be understood by examining three cognitive levels: surface or situation-specific negative automatic thoughts (NATS), cross-situational rules and assumptions (intermediate beliefs) and unconditional core beliefs. The deeper the cognitive level, the more difficult it can be to gain access to and change. However, it does not automatically follow that every client problem has to be viewed through these three levels or that the client will want to stay in therapy for deeper exploration of her problems once she starts feeling better; she may disagree that there are any underlying issues to resolve (e.g. 'I got what I came for'), and what was a collaborative relationship can turn into a coercive one if the therapist insists on the client staying in therapy for 'deeper work'.

The degree of complexity introduced into therapy is suggested by the clinical circumstances of each case, not by a predetermined view that every problem requires a depth-centred approach (see Point 15). For example, a client with panic disorder can use a well-established and empirically based treatment programme (e.g. Salkovskis and Clark, 1991) that is likely to help him become panic-free at the end of treatment and with his therapeutic gains being maintained at follow-up (Clark, 1996) without necessarily having to explore underlying (intermediate and core) belief levels as part of the programme. On the other hand, in working with clients with personality disorders (i.e. rigid personality traits: e.g. avoidant, dependent, histrionic; chronic maladaptive behaviour and poor interpersonal functioning), Young (1994, 2002; Young *et al.*, 2003) proposed a schema-focused approach with a 'primary emphasis on the deepest level of cognition, the early [childhood] maladaptive schema [core belief, e.g. 'I am bad']' (2002:

205). To promote client change at this level, therapy needs to be long-term with the length of treatment likely to take nine months or more (Davidson, 2000).

Within cognitive therapy there is disagreement about the use of and need for schema-focused approaches (working at the core-belief level) for clients with uncomplicated clinical problems which can be complicated by such approaches (James, 2001). For example, instead of being offered an anxiety management package to cope with major changes at work, a client suffering from acute anxiety about these changes is steered by an over-enthusiastic therapist into schema work which uncovers a core belief ('I'm no good') that the client neither knew he had nor sees the relevance of working on. This eagerness for schema-focused approaches 'is particularly worrying owing to the fact that, despite being far more intrusive, there is little evidence that they are more effective than non-schema interventions' (James, 2001: 404). Whether symptom reduction or elimination is sufficient help for the client or as a prelude to working at deeper cognitive levels, the level of clinical intrusion should match the requirements of the presenting problem, not the interests of the therapist.

17

CT is not interested in the client's past or childhood experiences

CT is an ahistorical (here and now) problem-solving approach: the client's distressing feelings are ameliorated by him identifying and changing his *current* maladaptive thinking and behaviour that serves to maintain these feelings rather than by him exploring unchangeable past events related to these feelings. However, clinical attention

> shifts to the past in three circumstances: when the patient expresses a strong predilection to do so; when work directed toward current problems produces little or no cognitive, behavioural, and emotional change; or when the therapist judges that it is important to understand how and when important dysfunctional ideas originated and how these ideas affect the patient today.
>
> (Beck, 1995: 7)

Clinical attention may shift to the past but it does not dwell there. With the client's 'strong predilection' for reflection, the therapist can help him to make connections with past adverse events (e.g. being 'betrayed by my best friend') to his current thinking about these events (e.g. 'I can't get over it. A best friend should never act like that'). When there is little, if any, therapeutic movement (e.g. the client expresses no sense of relief or freedom about leaving an abusive relationship) this may be due to the client being 'stuck' to a 'Why?' question (e.g. 'Why did I put up with it for so long? How can I be happy if I don't understand why?'). Looking back in order to answer these questions may not produce the satisfying answers the client is looking for, or, if satisfying answers are found, break the logjam in therapy: old questions may be answered, but new beliefs and behaviours are needed to avoid the possibility of the past repeating itself in the next relationship or impairing her new-found independence.

Sometimes the therapist will direct the client's attention backwards in order to help him see that what he considers to be 'true' about himself (e.g. 'I'm not good enough') was formed in response to being brought up in a highly competitive family environment where he was 'outshone' by his brothers; the legacy of that environment remains with him today in his endless striving to prove himself 'good enough' but, when falling short, confirms in his mind 'the truth about myself'. Teaching the client how he has maintained this core belief over the years can help him to see that his innate truth is no such thing but a long-standing, self-defeating belief that can be modified in order to help him develop a more realistic and compassionate self-image. While the learning history behind a client's dysfunctional beliefs may need to be explored, the 'crucial thing is for him or her to give up these currently held ideas so that tomorrow's existence can be better than yesterday's' (Grieger and Boyd, 1980: 76–77).

18

CT does not make use of the relationship as a means of client change

The standard view of the therapeutic relationship in CT is that it is necessary to help promote client change but not sufficient to produce optimum change – this is achieved through the execution of cognitive and behavioural techniques (Beck *et al.*, 1979; Beck *et al.*, 1985). These techniques are applied to the client's problems that occur outside of therapy, and only applied to the relationship itself when difficulties within it prevent the successful implementation of these techniques (these difficulties were called by Beck *et al.*, [1979] 'technical problems'). Later developments in CT viewed 'the relationship . . . as an intervention tool in itself' (Blackburn and Twaddle, 1996: 7). An example of the 'relationship as an intervention tool' is its use with clients who have personality disorders where the therapy relationship becomes 'a schema laboratory in which the client can safely evaluate maladaptive core beliefs' (e.g. 'No one can be trusted') (Padesky and Greenberger, 1995: 123; Beck, Freeman and Associates, 1990) and test out alternative and more adaptive core beliefs (e.g. 'Some people can be trusted sometimes'). Since clients with personality disorders often have difficulty in developing a therapeutic relationship, the 'laboratory' allows the therapist to observe the client's interpersonal functioning closely, 'as well as gaining a historical account of persistent difficulties in other relationships' (Davidson, 2000: 29).

Exploring interpersonal processes can help the therapist to understand and tackle the issues of transference, countertransference and impasses in the therapeutic relationship which hinder client progress (Wills and Sanders, 1997). Transference means how clients react (and, more importantly, overreact) to the therapist as they do to other significant people in their lives (Walen *et al.*, 1992). For example, the client may always defer to the expertise of the therapist, as she does to other authority figures in her life, instead of thinking things through for herself: 'My opinions don't count.' Such 'dependent thinking' will undermine the client's ability to become her own self-therapist – the ultimate goal of CT. The therapist can facilitate her movement towards more independent thinking by continually reinforcing the message that her 'opinions do count and that's why I want to hear your views'.

Countertransference is how the therapist thinks and feels about her client; e.g. she feels a sense of dread about the approach of the client's appointment time as she will have to endure 'an hour of moaning and whining'. With the help of a competent supervisor she can learn to endure each appointment without dread (e.g. 'The clients are not here to entertain me or make my life easy') and look for creative ways to shift the client from 'whining' about his problems to working on them. Impasses in the therapeutic relationship (e.g. disagreements over the pace of therapy) can be resolved through what Safran and Muran (2000) call 'metacommunication' – i.e. the client and therapist stepping outside of the strained relationship in order to comment upon it in a non-blaming spirit of collaborative inquiry (e.g. the therapist agrees to moderate his 'hurry up' approach to problem-solving and the client agrees to provide more specific information about her problem rather than keep talking in general terms about it). The therapist carries the main responsibility for initiating and maintaining the metacommunication process.

While the therapeutic relationship itself is not the primary means of client change in CT, it has become in recent years an important source of information about clients' interpersonal difficulties and a testing-ground for the development of more adaptive beliefs and behaviours.

19

CT is not interested in the social and environmental factors that contribute to clients' problems

This misconception assumes that CT takes the purely cognitive view that distorted thinking alone creates a person's emotional distress irrespective of his life circumstances (Gilbert, 2000); therefore, the client is to blame for his problems. Not so. CT is 'directed at correcting the combination of psychological and *situational* problems which may be contributing to the patient's distress' (Blackburn and Davidson, 1995: 16; emphasis added). Cognitive therapists investigate both worlds of the client, internal and external (the daily thought record [DTR] form requires situational information as well as thoughts and feelings; see Appendix 2). For example, with a client who felt 'trapped in an unhappy marriage and I've got to get out' the therapist would want to understand what makes the marriage unhappy for the client (e.g. 'My husband has become an alcoholic. I don't know him any longer and love has died') and what thoughts and feelings keep her 'trapped' within it (e.g. 'If I leave him, he'll just drink himself to death and I somehow think it will be my fault. I'll have killed him. I'll feel so guilty').

A ludicrous view of CT would be that the client is upset solely by her negative thinking about living with an alcoholic and that the debilitating effects of such a relationship have no effect on her psychological state. In real CT, the therapist would acknowledge the above client's dilemma and help her to question her guilt-related thoughts by conducting a realistic appraisal of her 'responsibility' for his death if she left him and her prediction came true: 'I have no more power stopping him from drinking himself to death if I leave him than I had stopping him drinking when I was living with him.' By moderating her guilt feelings, the client is able, with much sadness, to leave the relationship.

In essence, cognitive therapists want to understand, in collaboration with their clients, how objectively unpleasant situations can be made worse by the clients' distorted and unrealistic appraisals of these situations which then impair their ability to cope with them. Even in objectively very grim situations (e.g. a person is terminally ill), unrealistic thinking (e.g. 'This shouldn't be happening to *me*. I won't accept it') can prolong the person's anger and bitterness about his impending death and thereby obscure the fact that he has a choice regarding how he faces his death: his last months can be spent emotionally disturbed or living life to the full (Moorey, 1996).

Cognitive therapists are aware that practical help can sometimes be the best help (e.g. writing a letter to the local council in support of a client's rehousing application; facilitating a client's entry into a drug rehabilitation centre) in improving a client's environmental circumstances that hours of 'talk' may not deliver.

20

CT is just the application of common sense to clients' problems

This means that CT simply encourages clients to think realistically about their problems instead of blowing them out of proportion; once common sense thinking prevails, then emotional relief will be achieved. Beck's (1976) book, *Cognitive Therapy and the Emotional Disorders*, contains a chapter called 'Common Sense and Beyond' in which he says that each person 'by virtue of his personal experience, emulation of others, and formal education . . . learns how to use the tools of common sense: forming and testing hunches, making discriminations, and reasoning' (1976: 12–13). The therapist can encourage her clients to draw on their common sense in tackling their emotional problems.

However, common sense has its limits and fails 'to provide plausible and useful explanations for the puzzling emotional disorders' (Beck, 1976: 24). For example, a client may have had hundreds of panic attacks in which he believed that his pounding heart signalled an imminent heart attack but, on each occasion, no attack occurred. The client has a tremendous amount of evidence to disconfirm his catastrophic prediction but no such disconfirmation has taken place. Why has his common sense failed him so many times on this issue? Also, common-sense advice from his family and friends (e.g. 'If you were going to have a heart attack, you would have had one by now, so there's nothing to worry about, is there?') also fails to reassure him. To find the answer to this puzzle requires the uncommon sense of the therapist-as-detective uncovering the client's idiosyncratic view of the situation (i.e. why he continues thinking in the way that he does).

Salkovskis (1991) points to the importance of safety behaviours in maintaining anxiety and panic (i.e. behaviours which prevent the feared catastrophe from occurring). In the above example, when the client's heart is pounding he may relax, sit down, avoid exercise or strenuous activity in order to slow down his heart rate and thereby, in his mind, avert a heart attack. Unfortunately, his common-sense approach to saving himself actually strengthens or 'protects' his catastrophic predictions (e.g. 'That was a close one. Next time I might not be so lucky. I might die') because each panic attack is viewed as a 'near miss' (Wells, 1997) rather than a disconfirmation of these beliefs (the client believes he has had hundreds of 'near misses'). Once the client's internal logic related to his safety behaviours is revealed, he can drop these behaviours and undertake experiments (e.g. exercising when feeling panicky) in order to draw new and non-dangerous conclusions about his pounding heart (e.g. 'My heart is fine').

The client may reflect that what he has learnt in therapy 'just seems like common sense really', but it did not seem like common sense before he learnt it as he was initially fearful about dropping his safety behaviours and wondered if the therapist was 'mad' in suggesting it to him.

21

CT teaches clients to think rationally in tackling their problems

There is some truth in this. In recent years, cognitive therapies have been categorized as either 'rationalist' or 'constructivist' (Mahoney, 1988). The rationalist viewpoint

> is concerned with truth and logic, adopting the position that one's thoughts and feelings should correspond directly to external reality. In contrast, the constructivist viewpoint holds that an individual creates knowledge and that such knowledge corresponds to his idiosyncratic internal and independently existing reality. The emphasis is not on whether knowledge is accurate and true, but whether it is viable and adaptive.
>
> (Blackburn and Twaddle, 1996: 12)

Cognitive therapists who have been labelled as 'rationalist' have objected to this classification and claim that cognitive therapies fall along a rationalist–constructivist continuum rather than into an either/ or bifurcation: 'Thus therapists may espouse beliefs characterized by *both* the rationalist and constructivist position' (DiGiuseppe and Linscott, 1993: 119; emphasis in original). For example, in psychological disorders therapists want to understand the client's subjective construction of reality (e.g. 'I failed at important things in my life; therefore I'm a failure') and then help him to subject this belief to logical analysis (e.g. 'If your behaviour fails at important things in your life, how does the person fail as well?') and reality-testing (e.g. 'What evidence is there that you are a failure as a person?') – a shift from a constructivist viewpoint to a rationalist/empiricist one. Therefore, the cognitive therapist assumes the dual existence of a subjective and an objective reality (Alford and Beck, 1997): seeing the world through the client's eyes and then helping him to stand back from his upsetting thinking and use external reality as a standard against which to evaluate his distorted thinking (Vallis, 1991); e.g. the client realizes that if he was truly a failure as a person then he would fail at everything he has done, is doing or will do, and that this is patently false. Through this process the client is able to construct a more balanced and realistic appraisal of events (e.g. 'I have failed at some important things in my life but I'm not a failure as a person').

Clinical investigation of the client's maladaptive thoughts and beliefs is not solely rationalist/empiricist but also constructivist: for example, looking at the advantages and disadvantages of adhering to a particular belief (e.g. 'I must give a hundred per cent in everything I do'), and investigating the impact of a particular belief on a client's life (e.g. 'How does calling yourself a "failure" help you to cope constructively with setbacks?'), reflects a constructivist outlook (Blackburn and Twaddle, 1996), i.e. looking at the usefulness of such beliefs within the client's frame of reference rather than viewed against external reality; the client might conclude that such beliefs have outlived their usefulness and need to be modified. The use of the term 'maladaptive', which is ubiquitous in the CT literature, emphasizes 'the evaluation of clients' thoughts and beliefs in terms of *functionality* not rationality' (Clark, 1997: 92; emphasis in original); maladaptive is preferred to the term 'irrational' because 'at one time in the client's life these beliefs made sense' (Weishaar, 1993: 119) but now interfere with the client's well-being.

While CT does teach clients skills in rational thinking (some of the earlier daily thought record [DTR] forms, but not the one in Appendix 2, contained a column for 'rational responses' to automatic thoughts; later forms favour 'adaptive responses'), it emphasizes adaptive thinking to cope with adverse life circumstances, not clients becoming paragons of rationality. The last word on what CT actually is should be left to its founder, Aaron Beck. In a recent radio interview he said that teaching clients rationality in problem-solving 'is really an overstatement of what we really do'. CT is 'really what we call an empirical therapy: that a large proportion of the work that's done is actually experimental', i.e. testing out the client's fixed beliefs (e.g. 'I'm a loser') in order for the client to learn from experience: 'Cognitive therapy is also an experiential type of treatment . . . in that experience itself will reshape their beliefs if they [clients] will only open up the channels for new learning' (Persaud, 2003); so Beck's view is that CT is mainly empirical and experiential.

Part 3
CT PRACTICE

Getting started

22

Setting the scene

By setting the scene, we mean not plunging straight into therapy in order to 'get the client better' as quickly as possible but, instead, preparing the ground before the commencement of formal therapy. This involves welcoming the client in a courteous manner and engaging in a little chit-chat to break the ice (e.g. 'How was your journey?'). Clients can be asked if there are any initial questions they want to ask before the therapist starts to elicit their reasons for seeking counselling at the present time (e.g. 'I've had enough. I'll do whatever it takes to sort my life out', 'I want to see what therapy can offer', 'I do want to move forward but it's going to mean a lot of upheaval which I'm not sure about', or 'My wife's putting pressure on me to seek help. I don't think there's a problem'). Such reasons can help the therapist to assess each client's level of motivation to change (e.g., respectively, committed, curious, ambivalent and reluctant) and tailor the discussion to reflect it – for example, outlining a treatment plan for the committed, talking about the process and effectiveness of CT for the curious, looking at the pros and cons of change for the ambivalent, and examining whether a 'non-problem' (e.g. heavy alcohol use) might have some problematic features (e.g. deteriorating marital relationship) for the reluctant.

The therapist can ask clients about their expectations of therapy, which may vary considerably (e.g. 'You sort me out', 'You're going to explore my childhood and blame my parents for my problems', or 'You're going to pressurize me into doing things I don't want to do'), in order to deal with any misapprehensions they may have which can then lead into a brief description of CT: looking at the thought–feeling link, taking personal responsibility for change, setting an agenda, obtaining a specific problem focus, establishing clear, concrete and measurable goals, collaborating in problem-solving, carrying out homework tasks and becoming a self-therapist – the ultimate goal of CT. Client feedback is elicited about the CT model and then permission is sought to proceed with CT. Before permission is granted, the person is an applicant seeking help; after it, the person becomes a client who has made an informed choice.

The therapist can also discuss the tape recording of sessions and the rationale for them: as a cornerstone of supervision for the therapist in determining the quality of her work and enhanced and accelerated learning for the client by listening to the tapes between sessions – he may process information in the session poorly because of, for example, his emotional disturbance, his embarrassment about asking for clarification from the therapist or his preoccupation with how he thinks the therapist sees him (e.g. 'She thinks I'm weak and pathetic'). In our experience, the majority of clients agree to have their sessions taped and are not inhibited by or worried about the presence of the tape recorder in the counselling room (it is the therapists who are usually worried about taping sessions because they believe that their 'poor' therapy skills will be revealed in supervision).

The therapist can enquire if the client has been in therapy before (what kind?), and what was helpful (e.g. 'The therapist showed genuine interest in my problems. I really felt like I was cared about') and unhelpful (e.g. 'Therapy just seemed to wander everywhere. I felt lost') about it and if any therapeutic gains have been maintained (e.g. 'I felt a bit better afterwards but now I'm just as anxious as I ever was. I just gave up trying to change'). The therapist can use this information to help build a productive alliance with her client and flag up potential treatment obstacles (e.g. the client's lack of sustained effort). The issue of confidentiality and its limits needs to be discussed, i.e. who else will know about or have access to information regarding the client's problems (e.g. the therapist's supervisor, the GP who referred the client, other health professionals linked to the client's case). Practical issues like fees, timekeeping, treatment contracts if required, length and frequency of sessions, possible duration of therapy (based on regular progress reviews) are agreed upon.

The foregoing requirements for setting the scene might seem like a lot to do before formal therapy begins but it means that clients have a clearer picture of what lies ahead of them and have made an informed choice about proceeding with therapy; also, it might become clear that CT is not indicated for this client and he needs to be referred elsewhere.

23

Undertaking an assessment

The information gained from an assessment of the client's presenting problems forms the basis for developing an idiosyncratic case conceptualization (see Point 30). Wells (1997) suggests three main areas to cover in an assessment interview:

1 *A detailed description of the presenting problem.* This involves collecting data on the main thoughts, feelings, behaviours, physical reactions related to the presenting problem (depression triggered by the end of a relationship). Measures are used to assess the severity of the client's presenting problems (in this case, depression) and act as a baseline for, among other ways, determining the client's progress in therapy (e.g. are the scores coming down (progress) or going up again (setback or relapse)?). Two of the most commonly used measures in CT are the Beck Depression Inventory (BDI-II; Beck *et al.*, 1996) and the Beck Anxiety Inventory (BAI; Beck *et al.*, 1988). The BDI is a 21-item self-report inventory which provides a rapid assessment of the severity of the client's depression, including the degree of hopelessness experienced and the presence of suicidal ideas. The BAI is a 21-item self-report scale measuring the severity of the client's cognitive and physiological responses to anxiety.

2 *An ABC analysis of the problem.* This looks at a specific example of the problem in terms of A = antecedents or situations; B = appraisals and beliefs; and C = emotional and behavioural consequences.

(A)	(B)	(C)
At home alone, reflecting on the end of the relationship	'I don't deserve this. Why did he leave me? I can't be happy without him.'	Depressed and tearful

53

A client's emotions are best understood and most intensely felt in specific, not general, contexts. The ABC model provides a simple but powerful demonstration of the way thought influences and maintains feeling. More ABC examples can be collected to determine if there are patterns or themes emerging in the client's appraisals and beliefs (e.g. fear of social isolation).

3   *A longitudinal (historical) analysis.* This seeks to understand how past factors (e.g. a series of failed relationships, poor coping when living alone, depressive episodes, desperation to find new partners, strategies to try and prevent relationships failing such as being submissive and eager to please) have contributed to the client's vulnerability in life (seeing herself as worthless without a partner) and its relationship to her present problem.

Assessment evolves into a case conceptualization (see Point 30) as the therapist and client discuss how past and present interact to produce the latter's current difficulties and seek to devise an appropriate treatment plan to tackle her problems and achieve her goals. Beck (1995) suggests educating clients about their emotional disorders such as depression or panic so that their presenting problems can be attributed to the disorder rather than to themselves for being 'defective' or 'mad' (e.g. 'It's a relief to know that my problems are common and I'm not all alone in the world with them').

24

Assessing client suitability for CT

Even though cognitive therapy 'has become the single most important and best validated psychotherapeutic approach' (Salkovskis, 1996: xiii), not every client will be interested in this approach; nor will they necessarily like it or benefit from it. Safran and Segal (1990) developed a ten-item Suitability for Short-Term Cognitive Therapy Rating Scale by rating clients on a 0–5 scale, where a total score of 0 indicates least suitability and a total score of 50 the greatest suitability for short-term cognitive therapy. We now show how these ten items were used to assess the suitability for short-term cognitive therapy of a client who presented with several emotional problems related to increased pressures at work following company restructuring.

1   *Accessibility of automatic thoughts.* After an explanation and examples of what automatic thoughts are (see Point 3), is the client able to detect and report them? Yes. (4)

2   *Awareness and differentiation of emotions.* Is the client aware of and can distinguish between, for example, her anger, guilt, shame and depression? Partly: she has difficulty in being aware of and distinguishing between shame and guilt. (3.5)

3   *Acceptance of personal responsibility.* The client did accept personal responsibility for change but said 'I really wouldn't have these problems if it wasn't for my boss.' (3)

4   *Compatibility with the cognitive rationale.* The client understood and generally agreed with the cognitive model, including the importance of carrying out homework assignments. (4)

5   *Alliance potential (in session).* Can the client form a productive working alliance with the therapist? The client took umbrage at some of the therapist's questions (e.g. 'What do you mean how do I make myself angry when my boss asks me to stay late to finish a project?'), which might mean a less than optimum alliance potential. (3.5)

6 *Alliance potential (outside of session)*. Is the client able to form productive, positive relationships in her life? There was a mixed picture on this issue (e.g. she had close relationships with others but these could quickly unravel if she suspected disloyalty or lack of respect). (3)

7 *Chronicity of problems*. How long has the client had the problem? The client admitted to long-term dissatisfactions in life but the specific problem she wanted to focus on was of recent onset. (4)

8 *Security operations*. To what extent might the client engage in behaviour (e.g. avoidance) that keeps her safe in her own mind but prevents her from constructively tackling her problems? The client said she would be willing to 'meet the problem head on'. (5)

9 *Focality*. Is the client able to focus on the problem targeted for discussion? The client was able to do this with only occasional prompting from the therapist to 'keep on track'. (5)

10 *Client optimism/pessimism regarding therapy*. To what extent does the client believe that therapy will be able to help her? The client said she was 'hopeful. I know I've got to sort myself out.' (4)

The client's score was 39, making her very suitable for short-term cognitive therapy. Safran and Segal (1990) provide no cut-off point of unsuitability for short-term cognitive therapy; they merely state that high ratings indicate a good prognosis for therapy and low ratings indicate a poor prognosis. The client agreed to a provisional duration of therapy lasting ten sessions, with progress reviews every three sessions. No rating scale is infallible or the person administering it, so it might become evident several sessions into therapy that the person is actually unsuitable for short-term cognitive therapy (e.g. 'I initially liked the structure of cognitive therapy but now I realize that I want to talk about and deal with my problems without any constraints like agendas, thought forms or homework'). We have encountered some clients who want to modify CT to the point of unrecognizability (idiosyncratic adaption that is just too idiosyncratic!) and a referral elsewhere has been the agreed option.

Cognitive therapy is suitable for long-term work with clients such as those with personality disorders, but change will be slower as these clients have, *inter alia*, rigid and long-standing maladaptive beliefs that will be more difficult to modify; there are also likely to be more interpersonal difficulties in developing a collaborative relationship with the therapist, and the long-term use of avoidance strategies to block painful feelings and thoughts can be difficult to overcome. Davidson (2000) suggests that in working with personality disorders it is likely that therapy will take nine months or longer.

25

Structuring the therapy session

This means that each therapy session, following on from the assessment of the client's problems (see Point 23), will follow a predictable pattern. This pattern is explained to the client as part of his continuing socialization into CT (see Point 22). The therapist can say something like this:

> The session starts with finding out how you have been feeling in the last week and anything that may have happened during the past week you want to bring up. We'll look at your scores on any forms that you've filled out [e.g. Beck Depression Inventory and Beck Anxiety Inventory] and see what's going on there. I'd be interested in any feedback you have from the previous session. Then we can set the agenda [see next point] so the session remains problem-focused. Okay?

These pre-agenda setting items should be kept to a brief discussion (no more than a maximum of ten minutes), as the main focus of the session is working through the agenda; the therapist can encourage the client to be succinct in his replies to these items by asking very specific questions, such as 'How has your anger been in the last week?', rather than 'How have you been feeling in the last week?' which can result in a lot of detail not relevant to the client's problem. If an issue does emerge that either the client or therapist wants to explore further (e.g. the client says that his partner is threatening to leave him and he is very upset about it or that therapy is not helping him; the therapist notes an increase in the client's depression inventory scores while the client's report of his mood suggests an improvement in it), then this issue can be put on the agenda, not discussed independently of it. If the client expresses any suicidal ideas, these become the *immediate* agenda.

Structuring the session is a skilful and disciplined procedure to carry out and, in our experience, therapists, both novice and experienced, often neglect to do it in their eagerness to 'get at' the client's problem or because of their unease at placing a 'straitjacket' on the session (in the latter case, the session is usually less productive as discussion of the client's problem becomes diffuse rather than remains focused).

26

Setting the agenda

An agenda is a short list of items that will be the focus of that particular session. Setting an agenda is deemed by cognitive therapists to be the best way of making the optimum use of the therapy hour (though clients who have been in non-directive forms of therapy may become irritated at what they see as restrictions on their freedom to wander mentally; the therapist may need to explain patiently and repeatedly the rationale for agenda setting). The agenda items are jointly agreed (though reviewing and negotiating homework are permanent fixtures on the agenda). A typical agenda looks like this:

- Reviewing homework – what learning did the client extract from carrying out his homework assignment? (See Point 66.)
- Working on the client's prioritized problem and other problems if there is time.
- Negotiating new homework – what goal-relevant assignment does the client want to execute in the next week? (See Point 65.)
- Summarizing the session – initially, this is done by the therapist but is gradually transferred to the client as he gains competence and confidence in his developing role as a self-therapist.
- Feedback – what did the client find helpful and unhelpful about today's session? The client's reply to that last question should be greeted non-defensively by the therapist.

The last three items can take from 10–15 minutes to complete so it is important that the therapist keeps an eye on the time to prevent the session overrunning or the squeezing of these items into the few remaining minutes of the session. Also, there may be too many problems to be worked on so these need to be prioritized (usually one or two problems per session is enough), and when a problem is discussed the therapist should help the client to elicit and modify 'hot' (emotionally charged) thoughts connected to it, not just elicit the thoughts themselves or become entangled in excessive detail about the problem. Agenda-setting keeps both the therapist and client on track in developing ways to identify and modify key dysfunctional thoughts and beliefs and counterproductive behaviours that maintain the client's emotional difficulties.

27

Drawing up a problem list

Clients usually present with more than one problem. Listing the problems the client wants to work on emphasizes collaboration and reduces the likelihood of therapy drifting into clinically unproductive areas. The list can be 'ticked off' as progress is made on each problem. A problem list drawn up in the initial stages of therapy is not fixed for the remainder of it: problems can be added to or deleted from the list. The priority given to each problem is achieved through collaboration, unless the client is expressing suicidal ideas and/or intent which means this becomes the immediate clinical priority. The problem list is incorporated into the case conceptualization, along with the goals (see next point) and treatment plans (see Point 31). If the client has multiple discrete problems, the link between these problems in the case conceptualization may be tenuous or even absent; therefore each problem may need its own assessment and the therapist should indicate in the conceptualization that they are not related to one another.

Sometimes a client will present with a large number of problems that can leave both client and therapist feeling overwhelmed. I (MN) once saw a client who read out her problems from a notebook – the final count was fifty-three! However, it quickly became apparent as I was listening to her that her anxiety in various situations was linked to a fear of incurring the disapproval of significant others in her life which would then activate her core belief that she was inferior. As Fennell observes:

> The problem list . . . imposes order on chaos. A mass of distressing experiences is reduced to a number of relatively specific difficulties. This process of 'problem-reduction' is crucial to the encouragement of hope, since it implies the possibility of control.
>
> (Fennell, 1989: 179)

Sometimes all the problems listed are actually different aspects of a single problem (Fennell, 1989), and when this problem is addressed these aspects are also being ameliorated. On the other hand, there may be multiple problems that require treatment in their own right (Wells, 1997) as when a client presents with depression over losing his job, marital difficulties, heavy drinking since the loss of his job, anxiety in social situations, anger at discovering his son's illicit drug use and guilt because he sees himself as a poor role model for his children. The client can choose what he considers to be the most pressing problem to tackle (e.g. finding another job) or one that might prove easier to address (e.g. reducing his alcohol consumption): the latter option can engender confidence in him that other more difficult issues (e.g. his relationships with his wife and children) are also solvable and make him aware that his job-seeking attempts are likely to be impaired by his heavy drinking.

28

Agreeing on goals

We say 'agreeing on goals' because the therapist does not automatically go along with the client's goal selection. The client might select a goal that is outside of her control (e.g. 'I want my husband to come back to me'), counterproductive (e.g. 'I want to feel nothing when people hurt or criticize me') or unrealistic (e.g. 'I never want to *ever* experience another panic attack'). For each problem on the list there will be a specific goal. Wells suggests:

> Once problems have been prioritised they should be *reframed* as goals. The problem list provides details of '*what is wrong*' and this should be changed into a goal or a statement of '*what the patient would like to happen*'. Goals should be *operationalised* [made therapeutically useful] in concrete terms.
> (Wells, 1997: 51; emphasis in original)

Clients are prone to state their goals in vague (e.g. 'I want to feel less disconnected from myself') or general terms (e.g. 'I want to be happy in life'). The therapist would need to ask each client what specific changes would have to occur in order for these goals to be operationalized (e.g., respectively, 'I want to be more assertive at home in speaking up for what I want' and 'I want to be in a relationship'). The next step is to decide how progress towards these specific goals can be assessed or measured (e.g., respectively, keeping a diary recording her assertiveness at home and joining a dating service). Fennell (1999) suggests SMART criteria for goal-setting:

Simple and specific – 'I want to be able to go to the high street on my own'
Measurable – currently housebound; house to high street progress can be assessed in stages
Agreed – yes

Realistic – the client believes she has the ability to achieve this goal which is within her control

Timescale – this goal seems achievable within the time the client has allotted to stay in therapy

Goals should be stated in positive terms (e.g. 'I want to overcome my fear of public speaking') instead of negative terms (e.g. 'I don't want to feel so anxious and awkward when talking to a group of people') so 'that it is explicit what the patient is moving *towards* rather than away from' (Kirk, 1989: 41; emphasis in original). This helps the client to see new possibilities in her life rather than continually discussing her difficulties in each session. Additionally, goal-setting 'reinforces the notion that the patient is an active member of the therapeutic relationship, and that full involvement is required: the patient will not be "done" to' (Kirk, 1989: 41). Goals are flexible, not fixed, and can change in the light of incoming information (e.g. from homework assignments) that the client's initial goal was too ambitious, given the long-standing nature of her problems, or that she wants to capitalize on the unexpected quick progress she is making by now selecting a more ambitious goal.

29

Teaching the cognitive model

During the first session of CT it is important for the therapist to orient her clients to the thought–feeling link; in other words, to teach the cognitive model. The therapist's clinical judgement can determine the best time or moment to introduce the model. For example, the client might attend the appointment in an anxious state and it may be productive for the therapist to elicit then and there her client's anxiogenic thinking: 'What thoughts are going through your mind right now to make you anxious about coming here?' The client might reply: 'I'm worried you're not going to be able to help me and I'll never get better.' The therapist can ask her client what thoughts would reduce his anxiety: 'I suppose if I thought you could help me and there was hope for me after all.'

During the session the client might fall silent, become tearful or angry, stare at the floor. Such moments can become opportunities for teaching the model by exploring the client's thinking with a 'What's going through your mind right now?' type question. Writing the thought–feeling link on a whiteboard or flip chart can help the client to step back from his upsetting thoughts and feelings in order to make the cognitive model more concrete, vivid and understandable. The above examples are meant to teach the model through the use of questions so that the client makes the thought–feeling connection himself rather than being told by the therapist.

The therapist can take a didactic stance in teaching the model. You feel the way you think (Burns, 1999) might be the starting point: 'Let me explain what I mean by that statement by giving you an example. Two men are very keen on the same woman. They both ask her out and she rejects both of them. Now it's the same situation for both of them, rejection, but one man becomes depressed because he tells himself he's not attractive and no woman will ever want him while the other man is disappointed because he tells himself it's unfortunate he didn't get to go out with her but it's no big deal to be rejected. It's not the situation that makes each man feel the way that he does, but how each man *interprets* the situation that influences how he feels. That is the essence of the model: you feel the way you think.' The therapist can then show her client how the model can be used to understand his emotional reactions to life events, e.g. the client says he is anxious in social situations because he fears people will find him boring and avoid him. As Blackburn and Davidson point out:

> The therapist would indicate how the interpretation was congruent with the feeling but not necessarily the only interpretation possible. Such examples from the patient's own experiences would lead the therapist to demonstrate how cognitive therapy is relevant for the individual and might help to overcome his dysphoric moods.
>
> (Blackburn and Davidson, 1995: 56)

It is important for the therapist to remember that the client might understand the model but not agree with it (the mistake is to assume understanding for agreement); therefore, any reservations about or objections to the model need to be elicited (e.g. 'The model doesn't make any sense if you're in a concentration camp or dying of a terminal illness, does it?') and addressed (respectively, see Points 1 and 19). The client does not have to have complete conviction in the model to benefit from therapy: he can make progress despite some doubts about the model's applicability to every situation in life. Teaching the cognitive model is not a 'one off' but is done frequently throughout the course of therapy, with the client taking increasing responsibility for making the thought–feelings links and demonstrating to himself that by changing his upsetting thinking he is able to ameliorate his dysphoric moods.

30

Developing a case conceptualization

A case conceptualization is an individualized and hypothesized understanding of a client's problems within the cognitive model of emotional disorders; in essence, it seeks to pinpoint the factors that maintain the client's current problems and uncover the underlying factors that predispose her to experience these problems (see Appendix 1). Persons *et al.* (2001) describe the case conceptualization (or case formulation as they call it) at three levels:

1. The case – to understand the 'entire case as a whole, particularly the relationships among the patient's presenting problems and the schema [core beliefs] that appear to underlie many or all of the problems' (2001: 29).
2. The syndrome or problem – a specific syndrome or problem such as depressive symptoms, social phobia, bulimia.
3. The situation – a specific example of the problem in order to collect information about the client's thoughts, feelings and behaviours in that situation.

These three levels can be tied together in the following example: a client who presents with depression and withdrawal triggered by the end of a relationship (e.g. 'Why did he leave me? My life is meaningless without him. What did I do to drive him away? I can't face seeing anyone without him') may point to underlying intermediate beliefs (e.g. 'Unless I'm in a relationship, my life has no meaning') and core beliefs (e.g. 'I'm nobody on my own') which are long-standing cognitive vulnerability factors activated by the current stressors in the client's life. These therapist-driven hypotheses will need to be confirmed, modified or rejected based on information collected during the course of therapy.

The case conceptualization serves as the basis for an idiosyncratic treatment plan and guides therapy as in the above example: the client may wish to learn how to be relatively happy and independent by living on her own in order to give meaning to her life in the absence of a relationship and learning that she will always be a somebody whether or not she is in a relationship; the homework assignments will be directed towards achieving these goals. Without the conceptualization, techniques and interventions are likely to be used in a 'hit or miss' way because the therapist has rushed into treatment based on a cursory understanding of the client's problems. Beck (1995) likens therapy to a journey with the conceptualization as the road map and the client's goals as the final destination.

A case conceptualization is started in the first session and is continually refined/modified in the light of new information until therapy is terminated. Wills and Sanders (1997) suggest that a good case conceptualization helps the client to answer such questions as 'Why me?', 'Why now?', 'Why doesn't the problem go away?' and 'How do I get better?' The therapist shares the conceptualization with his client to determine its accuracy as well as to help the client understand herself and her problems better (Beck, 1995).

A case conceptualization approach differs from a psychiatric diagnosis by trying to understand the client's internal reality rather than attaching a label to it (e.g. obsessive-compulsive disorder, panic disorder, major depressive disorder): describing the clinical features of a psychological disorder does not tell the therapist much about the unique aspects of how the person experiences the problem. For example, two clients may both be diagnosed as having social phobia and therefore appear to have very similar or even identical problems; however, a case conceptualization approach might reveal different reasons for the development and maintenance of each person's social phobia thereby necessitating different treatment plans (Bruch, 1998). However, a diagnosis based on the criteria for each disorder in the *Diagnostic and Statistical Manual of Mental Disorders*, 4th edition (DSM IV; American Psychiatric Association, 1994) is usually included in the case conceptualization (e.g. Beck, 1995; Persons *et al.*, 2001) as an accurate diagnosis will help the therapist in formulating the conceptualization and devising treatment plans flowing from the diagnosis, but the case conceptualization personalizes the diagnosis and tailors the treatment plan to the client's idiosyncratic requirements.

Even though we stress idiosyncratic case conceptualization, in recent years cognitive therapists have developed some disorder-specific models, such as Clark's (1989) cognitive model of panic disorder (see next Point), which in many cases fit the clients' conceptualization of their problems and guide the therapist in understanding them (e.g. 'That's right. When I get all sort of spacy and feel unreal, I do think I'm going mad, losing control of my mind. How did you know that?'). Such CT generated conceptualizations have been called 'ready-to-wear' (Wills and Sanders, 1997) to distinguish them from bespoke ones.

31

Developing treatment plans

A treatment plan is derived from the client's case conceptualization and provides an overall view of how the client can free himself from the 'grip' of the disorder and achieve his therapy goals. The treatment plan is composed of a series of interventions that will modify those factors maintaining the client's disorder (if a client objects to the term 'treatment plan' as it sounds too medical, the therapist can substitute 'action plan'). Leahy and Holland (2000) state that treatment interventions need to be empirically validated and disorder specific (though an empirically validated treatment will be of little use to the client if the therapist lacks skill and creativity in implementing it). For example, Clark's cognitive model of panic states

> that individuals experience panic attacks because they have a relatively enduring tendency to interpret a range of bodily sensations [e.g. racing heart, breathlessness] in a catastrophic fashion . . . [this] catastrophic misinterpretation involves perceiving these sensations as indicative of an *immediately* impending physical or mental disaster [a racing heart will result in a heart attack; breathlessness will lead to suffocation].
>
> (Clark, 1989: 57; emphasis in original)

The treatment programme derived from this model has been empirically validated (Clark, 1996) and aims to help clients change their interpretations of bodily sensations from catastrophic to benign and modify the processes that maintain these catastrophic interpretations. Cognitive interventions include teaching clients the cognitive model of panic, examining the evidence for their catastrophic interpretations (e.g. 'My heart was banging so loud. It can't possibly stand the strain of that'; 'I couldn't get my breath. The pressure in my chest was so tight') and then examining the evidence for alternative, benign explanations of their bodily symptoms (e.g. 'When you're anxious, your heart rate speeds up. Your heart was designed to deal with a great deal of stress and strain without damaging itself'; 'Breathlessness is caused by over-breathing; it does not mean you're suffocating. You always get air no matter how bad you feel').

Behavioural interventions include panic induction (inducing feared bodily sensations by running on the spot for several minutes or deliberately hyperventilating), in order to teach clients that their panic sensations are not dangerous, and dropping safety behaviours (like avoiding exercise or trying to control one's breathing) in order to disconfirm catastrophic predictions.

Does this treatment programme produce a successful outcome for clients? Clark states that 'controlled trials indicate that this specialized form of cognitive therapy is a specific, and highly effective, treatment for panic disorder' (1996: 339); i.e. the majority of clients at the end of treatment are, and remain at follow-up, panic free. Other disorder-specific treatment programmes include those for obsessive-compulsive disorder (Salkovskis, 1999), post-traumatic stress disorder (Ehlers and Clark, 2000) and social phobia (Clark and Wells, 1995). For a discussion of empirically validated CT treatments, see Lyddon and Jones (2001).

Ways of
detecting NATS

32

Detecting NATS

As we discussed in Point 3, NATS are situation-specific involuntary thoughts that 'pop into' a person's mind at times of stress or emotional tension. They usually lie on the fringe of consciousness, or just outside of it, and can relatively easily be brought into the client's awareness by the client asking herself the 'cardinal question of cognitive therapy: What was just going through my mind?' (Beck, 1995: 10). Some clients can report their NATS without any prompting from the therapist while other clients may be 'completely unaware of them; they are so much a part of his [the client's] view of himself and the world that they do not appear distorted or problematic' (Persons, 1989: 116). Clients are often more aware of how they feel (e.g. 'I was terribly irritable all morning') than the thoughts connected to the feelings (e.g. 'I can't put my finger on why I was feeling like that'). NATS are the first type of thoughts that clients are taught to identify and evaluate as they are the easiest to detect and modify.

While we emphasize detecting NATS, clients can also experience self-defeating PATS (positive automatic thoughts). Some examples: a person with a past history of alcohol abuse decides to start drinking again (e.g. 'A couple of drinks won't hurt. I'll feel great. I deserve a treat. Yeah, go for it!'); a person in the manic phase of bipolar disorder (manic depression) makes grand, impulsive plans (e.g. 'I'll cash in my life savings. Buy a new sports car. Drive all around the country non-stop. I'll be as free as a bird'); a person with bulimia nervosa convinces herself that she can eat what she wants because 'I won't gain weight as I'll make myself sick afterwards' (Cooper *et al*., 2000). PATS also need to be detected, examined and modified.

In this point and the following ones (33–48), we will look at some of the main ways of detecting NATS. Asking direct questions is the most straightforward way of eliciting NATS. For example: 'What was going through your mind at that moment to make you so nervous when your boss asked you take over an important project?' This approach can quickly establish if the client has the ability, at the present time, to detect such thoughts. The client's introspection can be aided by the therapist's clear and specific questions (as above) rather than by vague and rambling ones (e.g. 'In that situation where you were getting nervous, what do you think you were thinking when your boss asked you to take over the project that led you to be so nervous. So what thoughts were you having then?').

Evocative questions can 'prise loose' some NATS when a client has responded with 'I don't know' to initial enquiries. For example, when a client says he does not know what goes through his mind to make him very anxious when he is the centre of attention, the therapist asks: 'What thoughts go through your mind at that very moment when all eyes are on you, *scrutinizing* you, *judging* you?' The client, who was now anxious, replied: 'They'll see me as a fat, undisciplined slob and despise me.' The therapist's evocative question was based on a hypothesis she had developed from information collected during the assessment of the client's problem.

With a client who is completely unaware of his NATS because they are a natural part of his world-view (see p. 77, Persons, 1989), questions can help to reveal them by the client imagining himself not acting in accordance with his world-view. For example, a client says that he puts himself at the back of any queue in life – 'That's just the way I am.' The therapist asks: 'Just imagine putting yourself at the front of the queue for a change. What thoughts would be going through your mind if you did that?' The client's reply reveals his NATS: 'I would be selfish for doing that. It would mean that my needs are more important than other people's. I'd be getting above myself. I don't deserve to put myself first.'

33

Guided discovery

Guided discovery is based on asking the client a series of questions in order to bring information into her awareness. Guided discovery is also known as Socratic questioning as it is derived from the method of teaching employed by Socrates consisting of asking questions to promote reflection which, in turn, will produce knowledge (see Point 60). Socratic questioning is driven by the therapist's genuine curiosity to understand the client's viewpoint, not a manufactured curiosity that wearily assumes he is going to hear all the expected answers. Beck *et al.* point out that 'questions should be phrased in such a way that they stimulate thought and increase awareness, rather than requiring a correct answer' (1993: 103). Also, guided discovery through Socratic questioning enables the client to provide her own answers rather than rely on the interpretations that might be offered by the therapist which can put the client 'in a compromising position – in that it is simpler to agree than to disagree, or to seem ungrateful or difficult' (Blackburn and Twaddle, 1996: 8–9). If the client does believe she is in a 'compromising position' she may be reluctant to reveal additional thoughts that might be more pertinent to understanding her presenting problems.

As Socratic questioning requires clients to *think* about their answers, the therapist should be wary about responding too quickly to the client's seeming inability or struggle to answer the question as premature intervention 'interrupts the client's thought processes and disrupts the purpose of the Socratic question' (DiGiuseppe, 1991a: 184). In our experience, responding too quickly is often based on the therapist's awkwardness with protracted silences or her impatience with the client's perceived slowness in 'moving therapy along'. In the following example, the therapist uses guided discovery in order to uncover the client's NATS:

Client: I'm sitting at home the other night, looking out the window at the rain and I started to feel really

	depressed. I don't know what was going on with me to feel like that.
Therapist:	Shall we find out? [client nods]. Can you remember what you were thinking as you were looking at the rain?
Client:	Just that it was a horrible night to be out and about.
Therapist:	Were you glad to be in then?
Client:	Yes, on that night but I always seem to stay in.
Therapist:	How come you 'always seem to stay in'?
Client:	Because I've got nowhere to go, no one to see [client's mood drops and she stares at the floor].
Therapist:	What does it mean to you that you've 'got nowhere to go, no one to see'?
Client:	That my life is dull and boring. I'm drifting along with no future, no prospect of happiness.
Therapist:	Are those the thoughts [NATS] that brought on the depression? [client nods]

It is important that the therapist does not guide the client to discover information that he wants found in order to confirm his hypotheses about her problems (e.g. 'Isn't it true that you always stay in because you believe you're unlikeable and want to avoid being rejected?'). Padesky and Greenberger (1995) call guided discovery 'a cornerstone of cognitive therapy', and it takes a lot of practice to be proficient in its use. Guided discovery is not only used to uncover NATS (and underlying beliefs) but also to construct alternative and adaptive thoughts and beliefs.

34

Using imagery

The term 'cognition' includes images as well as thoughts. Some clients might find it difficult to pinpoint their NATS in a specific situation, but the therapist can ask such clients if they had any pictures or images in their minds in that situation which might be more retrievable (e.g. 'I had an image of everyone turning their backs on me when I entered the room'). The client, in this example, can then be asked by the therapist what the meaning is that he attaches to the image in order to elicit his accompanying thoughts (e.g. 'I've lost their respect and I'll never get it back'). Using imagery can help clients to relive past situations in order to uncover the hot (emotionally charged) thoughts associated with these situations. For example, a client who said she felt anxious when walking in the high street, but did not know why, was asked to imagine the situation in the present tense as if it was happening right now:

Client: I'm walking down the high street. I feel very uncomfortable. I think everyone is looking at me, so I keep my head down.

Therapist: What would you be seeing if you put your head up?

Client: I always keep it down and just rush about to get my shopping over with as quickly as possible.

Therapist: But imagine putting your head up and looking around. What do you see?

Client: [becomes visibly tense] I see them staring at me, judging me. I hate it.

Therapist: What is it that they are judging?

Client: [becoming tearful] My looks.

Therapist: In what way?

Client: They think I'm ugly, hideous. I look like the elephant woman. They probably make jokes about me and have a good laugh. I can't bear it.

Therapist: Are those the thoughts that make you anxious when you go into the high street?

Client: [quietly] Yes.

Lazarus states that an 'understanding of the role that imagery plays in our daily lives provides a clue to unraveling otherwise insoluble puzzles' (1984: 20). Such a puzzle is when a client presents with a situation that he says he should be very happy about (e.g. getting married) but, instead, feels worried and standard CT questioning fails to elucidate his worry. To bring the client's worries into focus, the therapist can use the step-up technique (Lazarus, 1984) where the client visualizes his married life unfolding and the therapist keeps 'stepping-up' (moving forward in time) the image to the point where the worrying thoughts emerge: 'I can see it in my mind's eye now. Her irritating habits have become intolerable. I resent her more than I love her. She'll be destroyed if I leave her. So I'm trapped and unhappy.'

35

Making suggestions

No matter how skilful the therapist is as a Socratic questioner (see Point 33), there usually comes a point in therapy when the client responds with 'I don't know' and further questions from the therapist do not help the client to find ways of overcoming his cognitive roadblock. In order to tackle this roadblock, the therapist can make some suggestions based on the client's case conceptualization or derived from her clinical experience. In the following example, a client says 'I really have no idea why I feel so guilty if I spend time just reading a newspaper or watching television':

Therapist: [reading from the conceptualization] One of your underlying assumptions is 'If I don't have a real job then I'm not as good as others.' Now you've been out of work for several years due to illness and you said you try to cram a lot of activity into each day to prove that you are as good as others by having a job at home, so to speak; so do you see reading the newspaper or watching television as an indulgence, idling when you should be striving?

Client: Yes, that's exactly it now that you've mentioned it. It is an indulgence. I should be working hard to make up for not having a real job. I don't deserve any time to myself. I feel a failure if I don't complete my daily to-do lists. [The last four sentences are the client's NATS.]

In this example, a suggestion from the therapist provided the stimulus for productive introspection on the client's part; it would have been unproductive on the therapist's part to make further suggestions when the client was not in need of them (a surfeit of suggestions can help to induce passivity in a client as the therapist does most of her thinking for her). If the client had agreed with the therapist that she was indulging herself but provided no elaboration on her agreement, then the therapist could have asked: 'How does this indulgence lead you to feel guilty?' Such a question is designed to assess whether the client is being compliant with the therapist's suggestion (e.g. 'I was only agreeing with you. I don't want to appear difficult') or whether the suggestion has been genuinely helpful to the client in providing answers to her bafflement.

Another way of stimulating a client's introspection when he becomes stymied in pinpointing his situation-specific automatic thoughts is for the therapist to suggest a thought opposite to the client's expected response (Beck, 1995). For example, the client is uncertain why he feels so anxious about being asked out by a very attractive woman. The therapist says: 'You're anxious because you believe that she will see you as the perfect man for her.' The client replies: 'On the contrary. I think I'll disappoint her both in and out of bed. I won't live up to expectations [NATS].' The therapist can then tease out through Socratic questioning why the client thinks he will disappoint her and whose expectations he will not live up to – his own or what he imagines are her expectations of him.

36

In-session emotional changes

Changes in a client's emotional state can occur at any point in each session. The therapist needs to be alert to these affect shifts as they are important entry points into the client's thinking. These affect shifts can be obvious (e.g. becoming angry) or subtle (e.g. narrowing eyes). The client may be talking about an issue in a non-emotive way when the therapist notices something in his manner that she infers is an affect shift:

Therapist: That was quite a sigh. How are you feeling at this moment?

Client: Depressed.

Therapist: What thoughts are going through your mind right now to make you feel depressed?

Client: I've missed so many opportunities in my life, let them slip through my fingers. What a waste. Why didn't I grasp these opportunities and make the most of them?

Encouraging the client to answer his own question will help to make explicit the *meaning* implied by the question. Beck *et al.* stress the importance of ascertaining the meanings in clients' communications:

The *totality* of the meaning of the patient's experience is crucial. At times, the meanings people give to a situation may not be fully formulated but rather will have to be drawn out by the therapist . . . by relying exclusively on the immediate raw data of the automatic thoughts, the therapist misses the crucial – but unexpressed – meaning.

(Beck *et al.*, 1979: 30; emphasis in original)

The meaning of the client's last automatic thought is now ascertained by the therapist:

Therapist: What's your answer to that question?

Client: That I've always been a loser and always will be. I'll never amount to anything. My life is an endless catalogue of failure. [Client becomes tearful and stares at the floor slowly shaking his head]

The client's answer is filled with 'hot thoughts'. These are thoughts 'that are most connected to moods . . . [and] conduct the emotional charge' (Greenberger and Padesky, 1995: 55), and are the most important NATS to elicit and modify.

37

Finding the thoughts by ascertaining the client's idiosyncratic meaning of the event

Blackburn and Davidson point out that 'patients often talk about events as if they were the cause of their bad feelings. The therapist establishes the missing link (the interpretation) by *ascertaining the meaning of the event*' (1995: 73; emphasis in original). In the following example, the client believes the event made him feel guilty:

Event	Feeling
Arriving ten minutes late to pick up his sons from school	Guilty

The client supports his viewpoint by stating that if he got to the school on time then he would not have felt guilty, so 'it surely follows that the situation made me feel guilty because I turned up late'. In response to the therapist's enquiry, the client tentatively agrees that not every father (or parent) would feel guilty if he arrived late at the school to pick up his children. Having made this opening into his thinking, the therapist asks him what it means to him to turn up late at the school:

Event	Thoughts	Feeling
Arriving ten minutes late to pick up his sons from school	My boys were very worried when I wasn't there to pick them up. I shouldn't have worried them like that. I'm a bad father for putting them through that ordeal.	Guilty

Thus, the therapist demonstrates to the client that his feelings are mediated by his interpretation of the event and not directly caused by the event itself ('It makes sense. If I had arrived late and my boys were playing about enjoying themselves, then I would have felt relieved, not guilty').

38

Focusing on feelings

Beck has called emotion 'the royal road to cognition' (quoted in Padesky, 1993a: 404), and helping clients to activate and explore their feelings usually reveals important NATS. For example, a client who says he feels angry about his father's behaviour towards him but is reluctant to tell him is encouraged by the therapist to imagine that his father is sitting opposite him in the counselling room and to 'tell him how you're feeling':

Client: [talking to his father] I'm angry with you. I asked you out for a drink last Sunday and you said you were too busy. Why are you always too busy when I try and arrange something for us to do together? I feel you're always pushing me away from you. Why do you do this to me?

Therapist: Why do you think your father is always pushing you away?

Client: [becoming tearful] He doesn't love me. I'll never be good enough for him, unlike my brother. He'd disown me if he could. Nothing I do ever pleases him. [Hot thoughts]

The use of chairwork, as exemplified above, is usually associated with Gestalt therapy, not cognitive therapy. Cognitive therapists borrow techniques from other therapeutic approaches, but these techniques are used within the framework of the cognitive model of emotional disorders (Clark and Steer, 1996) – in the above example, to elicit hot thoughts.

Clients can keep a mood diary and note changes in mood in order to 'catch' their NATS. Michael Free likens catching NATS to hunting a very shy animal:

We have to find out about the AT's [automatic thoughts] habits. We can look for its tracks or droppings. With automatic thoughts

we can tell where they've been by the emotion they leave behind
. . . a stab of anxiety, a brief sinking feeling, a flash of anger. Be
on the look out for those signs and see if you can catch a glimpse
of the automatic thoughts. As you get used to it you will be able
to see more of the AT, until you are able to write it down in a
complete sentence.

(Free, 1999: 61)

For example, a client keeps a mood diary and notes momentary
panics when she is asked by her boss to undertake impromptu tasks
and 'glimpses' part of the automatic thought, 'Oh God!' Through
regular recording in her diary of these panics, and thereby becoming
accustomed to them rather than startled by them, she is eventually
able to see the full automatic thought(s): 'Oh God! I've got to use my
initiative. I'll make a mess of things. My boss will think I'm really
incompetent and regret promoting me.'

39

Assuming the worst

Wells states that 'one of the most effective questions for eliciting NATS in the therapeutic dialogue is '*What's the worst that could happen if. . .?*' (1997: 58; emphasis in original). Freeman *et al.* (1993) suggest that this question should not be asked unless the therapist believes that the client is capable of understanding the hypothetical nature of the question, of developing adaptive responses to highly adverse events and benefiting from the idea that 'If I can handle the worst, then I can handle anything else less than the worst.' Additionally, this question is indicated if the worst outcome is based on a highly distorted reading of future events such as 'My whole life will be totally ruined if I fail the exam' or 'I'll be so terrified of the plane crashing I'll be running up and down the aisles screaming and vomiting over everyone.' In the following example, a client with performance anxiety is asked to consider the worst:

Client: I'll give a terrible performance.
Therapist: That's a general description of your performance. What specific aspects of it are you most anxious about?
Client: I'll be so nervous talking to all those people that I'll become tongue-tied.
Therapist: What's the worst that could happen if you become tongue-tied?
Client: I'll just freeze up, nothing will come out of my mouth.
Therapist: Is that the worst that could happen?
Client: No. The worst thing is that I'll be exposed as a phoney and my professional credibility will be destroyed. [The client's key NATS or hottest thoughts have been identified]

Assuming the worst can also be undertaken if the client's imagined fear could occur and he wants to face it (e.g. terminal illness, the end of a long-standing relationship), or if the client avoids focusing on it directly but it continually distracts him in therapy, which the therapist points out: 'You are worried about your son's strange behaviour because you believe he's overfriendly with another man, but it seems to me that what you're most worried about is that your son may be gay, the unspoken but nagging subject in therapy. Is there any truth in this?'

40

In vivo **exposure**

In vivo exposure occurs when clients agree to face the feared situations they usually avoid in order to elicit their hot thoughts. In the safety of the counselling room the client may find it difficult to gain access to such thoughts because he is obviously not in the situation which triggers them, he may play down the distressing nature of the thoughts (e.g. 'I'm being silly really. I know nothing really bad is going to happen to me'), or he may have thought something 'terrible' was going to happen and quickly left the situation but now cannot specify what the 'terrible' event that he believed would occur was. By encouraging clients to enter into feared or avoided situations, their hot thoughts can be activated. For example, a client who is afraid of eating in public but cannot say why is accompanied to a local café by the therapist:

Client: I feel everyone's looking at me while I eat. I feel so tense. It's hard to chew and swallow my food.

Therapist: What do you think is going to happen if you stay here and continue to eat?

Client: I'm going to embarrass myself.

Therapist: In what way?

Client: I'll be so tense. I won't be able to get the food down and I'll start to choke on it. Then I'll spit it out or it will dribble out of my mouth. I'll make an awful spectacle of myself. People will be appalled at my behaviour and turn away in disgust. (The last four thoughts are the key NATS]

This exposure to a previously avoided situation yielded crucial assessment data that remained untapped while the client was sitting in the therapist's office. Accompanying clients on such trips early in therapy is often necessary as they are hardly likely at this stage to carry out such feared trips alone.

41

Role play

This is used when clients have difficulty revealing salient cognitions in their problematic relations with others. The therapist can play the person with whom the client experiences interpersonal difficulties. It is important that the therapist takes on the characteristics that the client ascribes to the other person if the role play is to have any verisimilitude (e.g. if the client says that a work colleague is rude and abrupt then the therapist *should not* play this person as polite and considerate as this will undermine the role play). In the following example, the therapist plays the role of the client's friend who is always critical of him and the client wants to know why he puts up with his friend's behaviour.

Therapist: You were supposed to pick me up at seven. Why the hell were you late?

Client: Sorry. I had trouble with the car.

Therapist: Don't let it happen again. Now I've been invited to a party this weekend. I suppose you want to come along.

Client: Yes, I would.

Therapist: You can drive me there and buy beers for the party, but don't get drunk because you'll be driving me home unless I get lucky with a couple of birds, then you can get lost. Okay?

Client: [becoming visibly tense] I wouldn't want to get in the way.

Therapist: [coming out of role] It seems like there's something you want to say but you're holding back.

Client: I want to tell the arrogant bastard to get stuffed!

Therapist: What stops you?

Client: I don't want to get kicked out of the group he's the sort of leader of.

Therapist: If you were kicked out, then what?

Client: [quietly] That would prove that no one likes me. I'd be a real sad case. I'd be drifting around the town with no one to talk to or hang around with [NATS].

Therapist: Is that why you put up with such behaviour then to avoid that outcome? [Client nods]

42

Analysing a specific situation

When a client talks about her problems in general terms it can be difficult for the therapist to tease out her NATS because concrete examples of the problems remain elusive. Also, emotions are more intensely felt in specific situations (e.g. 'I felt scared when it looked as if I was going to be late for the staff meeting') than they are at a general level (e.g. 'I'm concerned about my poor timekeeping'). For these reasons it is important for the therapist to anchor the general problem in a specific context:

> *Client*: There's no specific situation. I'm just a worrier. I always have been. End of story.
>
> *Therapist*: Are you worried at this particular moment? [client nods] What thoughts are going through your mind at this moment to make you feel worried?
>
> *Client*: What if you can't help me? What if therapy is a waste of time? Therapy might make me worse with you messing around with my mind [NATS].

Instead of seeing worry as amorphous, the therapist isolates and elicits from his client worrying thoughts related to coming to therapy and these provide the entry point to begin to understand her subjective experience. It is important to note that when a client verbalizes her thoughts as questions, as in the above dialogue ('What ifs . . .?'), the therapist needs to help the client to convert these questions into clear statements in order to remove any potential doubt or ambiguity: 'You won't be able to help me – like all the other therapists I've seen' and 'Therapy will be a waste of time and I might as well leave now.' Examining NATS is more effective when they are clearly expressed as this allows more helpful and adaptive responses to be developed to answer them.

43

NATS in shorthand

This means that NATS can be 'composed of just a few essential words phrased in telegraphic style: "lonely . . . getting sick . . . can't stand it . . . cancer . . . no good." One word or a short phrase functions as a label for a group of painful memories, fears, or self-reproaches' (McKay *et al.*, 1997: 20). Just as when they are phrased as questions (see Point 46), NATS phrased in a telegraphic style will be difficult to examine and respond to. In the following exchange, the therapist clarifies the client's shorthand replies:

Therapist: When you didn't get the promotion what thoughts went through your mind to make you feel angry?

Client: Typical . . . not again . . . why? That's what I was thinking.

Therapist: It is important for us to expand those words into sentences so we can get the full meaning behind the words. Okay? [client nods] Can you make it clear what you mean by 'typical'?

Client: Well, typical is typical. I don't know what else to say.

Therapist: Okay. Does it mean, for example, that your company was acting in its typical way of fairness and loyalty when you didn't get the promotion?

Client: Not likely! It's typical of the way those bastards do business: it's who you know, not what you've achieved, that gets you promoted [first NAT].

Therapist: What does 'not again' mean?

Client: This is the second time I've haven't got the promotion.

Therapist: And if that's true, what does that mean to you?

Client: There's a conspiracy against me in the company because I don't toe the line [second NAT].

Therapist: And can you expand on your third thought 'why'?

Client: Why me? They've got it in for me because I speak my mind and am not a brown-noser like some of my colleagues [third NAT].

It is important that the therapist does not assume she knows the meaning embedded in the client's telegraphic thoughts (e.g. 'Hmm . . . "Not again" . . . Injustice') otherwise she will be replicating his telegraphic style with the upshot that she and her client might be following different agendas. In order to avoid this outcome, the therapist needs to enquire about the meaning of the client's telegraphically expressed thoughts.

44

Symptom induction

In Point 40 we looked at encouraging clients to expose themselves to feared situations they usually avoid in order to reveal their hot thoughts. Wells explains that 'another type of exposure task depends on exposure to internal bodily cues. The elicitation of bodily sensations or cognitive symptoms that are the focus of preoccupation and/or misinterpretation can provide access to a wide range of cognitions concerning danger' (1997: 67). In panic disorder, clients fear arousing certain bodily sensations such as breathlessness, palpitations or dizziness as these signal an imminent disaster involving, respectively, suffocation, heart attack or fainting (see Point 31). Catastrophic cognitions can be elicited by encouraging clients to engage in interoceptive (physiologically arousing) exposure exercises like running on the spot, spinning in a chair, staring at bright lights, shaking one's head from side to side or hyperventilating (Barlow and Cerny, 1988). For example, a client who ran on the spot for one minute in the therapist's office revealed his panic-inducing thoughts: 'My heart can't take it. It's going too fast. I'm going to have a heart attack if I don't stop now!' (The therapist's prior consultation with the client's GP ascertained that the client had no genuine heart problems.)

One of the factors that maintains severe health anxiety (hypochondriasis) is selective attention to illness-related information (Salkovskis and Bass, 1997). The client's attention is focused on information that could be consistent with her illness beliefs, not on information that could be inconsistent with them. Self-focused selective attention experiments teach the client that focusing on normal, but usually unnoticed, bodily sensations (e.g. tingling, twinges, aches) increases not only her awareness of these sensations but also the intensity of the sensations; preoccupation with these sensations leads to the worrying conclusion that something could be seriously wrong with her such as 'This tingling means I'm getting multiple sclerosis' (hot thought).

45

Behavioural assignments

These can be used with any client problem (not just anxiety) where it is difficult to elicit the client's NATS. For example, a client said he would feel inexplicably sad if he cleared out the spare room of his old possessions, but 'I desperately need the room for a guest bedroom'. He agreed to start the task that weekend and record his thoughts on a Daily Thought Record (DTR) form (see Point 47). At the next session, he said that clearing out his 'old stuff' triggered pleasant memories of his younger days which he contrasted with the present: 'The happiest part of my life is behind me. Everything is dull and grey now. Where did my life go?' (NATS). Another client was procrastinating over writing an article for an academic journal but said he was baffled by his continuing delay in 'getting down to it'. He said that he would 'get down to it' that evening and record his accompanying thoughts. At the next session, his DTR form revealed he had become very angry imagining his finished article being rejected or being subjected to extensive revision: 'How dare they treat my work like this. Who are they to criticize me? They should automatically accept it after all my hard work. I'm not going to let those bastards pull me down to their level by tearing my article apart!' (hot thoughts).

Sometimes the behavioural assignment can be carried out in the session in order to uncover the client's NATS. A client agreed to start filling out her 'boring' tax self-assessment form but quickly became frustrated with the task, screwed up the form and threw it to the floor: 'It's so boring. I can't make head or tail of it. The damn form makes me feel I'm stupid' (hot thoughts). Another client who avoided cold-calling local businesses, even though it was a key way of selling himself to them as a stress management trainer, agreed to make a cold-call from the therapist's office. The call lasted a couple of minutes and the client put down the phone with a deep sigh and said 'they weren't interested'. When the therapist asked him what that meant to him, he said: 'I feel they are rejecting *me*, not just what I have to offer. Each rejection will ultimately destroy my confidence' (NATS).

46

Eliciting NATS from less important cognitive data

As David M. Clark has observed, not all automatic thoughts are clinically useful: 'Anyone who is at all distressed will have an enormous number of negative thoughts, most of which are totally irrelevant. They're sort of rubbish, really. They're not driving the system' (quoted in Weishaar, 1993: 112). Therefore, the therapist needs to sift through this cognitive outpouring carefully in order to pinpoint the hot (emotionally charged) thoughts that are 'doing the emotional damage'. For example, a client may provide reflections on his thinking in a particular situation rather than the actual thoughts – as this client does when he muses on a boardroom incident: 'Hmm. I think I was possibly anxious because I was wondering what the chairman thought of me when I didn't have the exact figures he wanted. It was something along those lines.' In order to uncover the actual thoughts, the therapist, through imagery, re-creates the boardroom incident in the present: 'Oh God! I've shown myself up as a complete incompetent. The chairman has lost all faith in me. That's the end of my career with this company.'

Clients can often readily report streams of thoughts connected to their difficulties but omit key disturbance-inducing NATS. In the following example, the client says she feels 'terribly guilty' about her daughter's behaviour, but guilt-inducing thoughts are not evident in the way she talks about the problem:

Client: I do feel terribly guilty about what my daughter is getting up to. You know, things like staying out late, bunking off school, mixing with bad company, won't do what I tell her to. I think to myself, 'Is she on drugs? What's going to happen to her if she keeps on like this?' These things are always on my mind. Maybe I should have it out with her once and for all. She's driving me around the bend.

Running parallel with this first stream of thoughts is a second one containing the client's appraisals of herself or the situation. The therapist helps the client to 'tune into' this second stream in order to locate her distressing thoughts:

Therapist: You said you felt terribly guilty about your daughter's behaviour. What thoughts make you feel so guilty?

Client: I didn't bring her up right. It's my fault that she behaves as she does. I'm a bad mother. If I'd been a good mother she wouldn't have turned out like this [key NATS].

Beck (1995) says that clients often report interpretations of their thoughts instead of the actual thoughts. For example, in response to the therapist's question of what goes through the client's mind each time she volunteers to work late, she replies: 'I'm overcompensating for previous career uncertainties' (interpretation). The client's 'previous career uncertainties' were a succession of 'going nowhere jobs. Now I know where I'm going I need to make up for lost time.' Armed with this information, the therapist asks: 'What thoughts drive you to make up for lost time?' The client replies: 'I've got to prove to people that I'm not a failure and that I haven't wasted my life' (NATS).

When clients are asked the 'What was going through your mind?' type of question, they frequently reply with rhetorical questions such as 'How could I have done that?', 'What's the use in trying?' or 'Why does this always happen to me?' Rhetorical questions are not real questions that seek information but are ones filled with emotion, and implicit in them are hot thoughts (Grieger and Boyd, 1980). The therapist helps each client to make his implicit hot thoughts explicit by asking him to answer his own questions: respectively, 'I did do that bad thing because I'm wicked' (guilt); 'There's no point in trying. Nothing ever goes right for me' (depression) and 'This always happens to me. It's the story of my life. It's not fair' (hurt).

47

Separating situations, thoughts and emotions

Cognitive therapy states that it is our interpretations of events rather than the events themselves that produce our emotional reactions, therefore it is important that clients make this connection if they are to profit from CT. When clients discuss their problems it is often in a jumbled manner (understandably so) with no clear separation between situations, thoughts and feelings, and they often blame the situation itself for how they feel, e.g. 'My husband makes me angry when he goes off to play golf every Sunday morning.' In order to illustrate to clients the mediational role of their thinking in producing their emotional reactions to events they are shown how to use the first three columns of the Daily Thought Record (DTR; see Appendix 2). The DTR is a five-column worksheet that helps 'clients learn to distinguish between situations, thoughts and feelings, identify inaccurate thinking, and develop more balanced appraisals' (Tinch and Friedberg, 1996: 1).

In the early sessions of therapy, clients are taught to focus on the first three columns (situations, thoughts, and emotions) in order to gain practice at detecting their negative automatic thoughts (NATS) and recognizing how they are connected to the distressing emotions they experience in specific situations; once clients are able to do this, they can then turn their attention to challenging their NATS. To return to the above example:

Situation	NATS	Emotion
Husband going off to play golf on a Sunday morning	'He should want to be with me but as he doesn't, this means he's stopped loving me. Why the hell is golf more important than me? I'm a golf widow and he doesn't give a damn.'	Angry

Clients are asked to rate the believability of their NATS and the intensity of their emotions using a 0–100 per cent scale. The client rated the believability of her NATS at 80 per cent and the intensity of her anger at 85 per cent. It is important that session time should be set aside to review clients' DTRs when they have completed them as part of their homework assignments.

DTRs should not be given to the client if she does not agree with the cognitive model (e.g. 'My husband makes me angry. That's the whole problem') or is unwilling to fill out the forms (e.g. 'I came here for help, not bloody form-filling'). Until such difficulties are dealt with, filling out the DTRs will have to wait. For example, the client did eventually see and accept the thought-feeling link by the therapist asking her how she would feel if her husband: (1) stayed at home with her on a Sunday morning and made a fuss of her ('Happy because he wants to be with me'), (2) stayed at home and read the newspaper ('Hurt because I don't deserve to be ignored'), (3) stayed at home but felt morose ('Guilty because I've stopped him doing what he really enjoys') and (4) stayed at home but only went through the motions of being pleasant to her ('Anxious because he resents me and therefore he might find someone else'). Filling out the DTR forms helped the client to take ownership of her thoughts and feelings rather than blaming her husband's behaviour for them. Beck *et al.* (1985) suggest encouraging clients to put their 'he/she/it makes me feel' statements into the active voice ('I make myself angry') rather than the passive voice ('My husband makes me angry').

Obviously it takes time and effort for clients to learn the differences between situations, thoughts and emotions, and mistakes frequently occur. For example, a client puts 'I feel anxious that I might not get the job' in the NATS column when, in fact, 'anxious' should go in the emotion column and 'I might not get the job' in the situation column (this is a realistic view of his job interview). In order to discover what his NATS are, the client needs to ask himself what it means to him if he does not get the job: 'No employer will ever want me. They know I'm useless. I'll never get a good job, only menial work.' Another example might be a client who puts 'trapped' in the emotion column after a row with her boyfriend (situation) when 'trapped' should go in the NATS column as it is a thought not an emotion ('I'm trapped in this relationship'). The client can then ask herself how she feels about being trapped in the relationship – 'angry' – which she then puts in the emotion column.

Distinguishing between thoughts and feelings

People frequently say 'I feel' when they actually mean 'I think', such as 'I feel that my son and me are slowly drifting apart' (watching soap operas, for example, shows how dominant are 'I feel' statements over 'I think' statements). People would probably be annoyed if they were frequently corrected when they misused 'I feel' statements: 'When you say "I feel that my son and me are slowly drifting apart" what you really mean is "I think that my son and me are slowly drifting apart".' However, in CT it is crucial to make such corrections (but not incessantly or condescendingly) because by modifying dysfunctional thoughts distressing feelings are ameliorated (emotions are hard to change directly but easier indirectly through changes in thoughts and behaviours); so clients need to learn to distinguish between genuine thoughts and feelings. Also, if this distinction is not made, clients will believe that their 'feelings' are being challenged when it is their thoughts that are actually being targeted for examination. As Walen *et al.* point out:

> Feelings are not open to dispute; they are phenomenological [subjective] experiences for which only the individual has data. You cannot argue with such subjective states, whereas thoughts, beliefs, and opinions are open to challenge.
>
> (Walen *et al.*, 1992: 98)

Greenberger and Padesky suggest as a general rule that 'moods [e.g. anxiety, depression, guilt, shame, anger] can be identified in one descriptive word. If it takes you more than one word to describe a mood, you may be describing a thought' (1995: 28). For example, a client might say 'I feel like I'll never be able to overcome this problem', which might be converted by the therapist as 'You have this thought that you will never be able to overcome this problem. How do you feel with that thought in mind?' The client might reply with another 'feel' statement: 'I feel that therapy won't be able to help me.' The therapist can point out that the client has now given her two thoughts and then ask again how he would feel with those thoughts in mind: 'Depressed.' It is important that clients express their thoughts in the first person singular, such as 'I'll always be a failure' or 'No one likes me', in order to claim authorship of these thoughts rather than distance themselves from them by using an impersonal voice: 'One would see oneself as a failure in those circumstances' or 'Everyone thinks at some time in their life that no one likes them' (Neenan and Dryden, 2000).

Some clients may use one word to describe their feelings, such as 'bad', 'crap' or 'shit'. Unfortunately, these kind of one-word descriptions, though vivid, do not pinpoint which one-word emotions cognitive therapists are looking for. By asking the client about his thoughts (e.g. 'I let down my best friend. He's always there for me') and behaviours (e.g. 'I keep on trying to make it up to him'), the therapist is able to pinpoint the client's 'shit' feeling as guilt. The client can then decide to use the term 'guilt' or stay with his own idiosyncratic usage.

Examining and responding to NATS

Answering back

Once clients have elicited their NATS and understood the differences between situations, thoughts and feelings, they are now ready to examine their NATS in various ways in order to develop more helpful and adaptive responses to them (see Points 50–62). Beck *et al.* state that 'the therapist's major task is to help the patient think of reasonable responses to his negative cognitions . . . to differentiate between a realistic accounting of events and an accounting distorted by idiosyncratic meanings' (1979: 164). As we have seen in the section on detecting NATS, idiosyncratic meaning (e.g. 'My life is over') can make dealing with an objectively unpleasant situation (e.g. losing one's job after twenty years with the same company) much more difficult (e.g. the client says he feels 'overwhelmed with sadness and despair'). Encouraging clients to look at the situation in more realistic ways reduces the intensity of their distressing feelings (e.g. 'My life with that company is over and I still feel upset about it, but not to the same extent as I did. I realize that my life still has new possibilities and opportunities if I want to seek them out'). In order to achieve this outcome, clients are taught to regard their NATS as hypotheses about themselves, others and the world so that they can be tested and evaluated (see Point 11). If a client's NATS are realistic (e.g. 'I have no friends'), then ways to tackle this situation would be developed.

Examining clients' NATS is *not* based on the therapist trying to prove to her client that his thinking is wrong while hers is right or the therapist adopting the role of a prosecutor in a courtroom and trying to 'catch out' the client when discussing his thoughts (e.g. 'You say you're all alone in the world but you told me earlier that neighbours pop in to see how you are and you get phone calls from your family. It's not true then, is it?'). Examination is based on collaborative empiricism, which is the therapist and client working together to test the validity and usefulness of the latter's NATS and generating alternative responses to the problematic situation.

50

Weighing the evidence

Weighing the evidence for and against a particular automatic thought 'is probably the most common method of cognitive restructuring [thought and belief change]' (Moorey, 1990: 240). For example, a client says that 'nothing ever goes right for me' and lists past and present setbacks and failures to support this thought, and cannot think of any contradictory evidence; in his mind, this 'proves my case':

Therapist: You said you've moved house recently. How did that go?

Client: It was all right.

Therapist: So did the house move go right for you?

Client: Yes, I suppose so.

Therapist: How long have you been married?

Client: Fourteen years.

Therapist: How would you describe those fourteen years?

Client: They've been happy most of the time. Okay, so you've found two things that have gone right for me and maybe there are other things I can't see at the present time. Am I supposed to suddenly become a positive thinker then?

Therapist: Positive thinking doesn't usually consider evidence but realistic thinking does. I want you to try and stand back from your thought, 'nothing ever goes right for me', and consider all the evidence, not just part of it (the therapist helps the client to uncover further evidence against the thought). How might you respond now to that thought?

Client: Well, I suppose it would be more accurate to say that 'Sometimes things go right for me and sometimes they don't and, therefore, it's important for me to keep things in perspective.' I'd feel a bit better if I can remember that.

Difficulties can arise over what constitutes evidence: typically, the therapist is seeking facts to support, modify or disconfirm her client's thoughts while he is furnishing information based on 'gut feelings' or assumptions. Newman (1989) suggests which information can qualify as objective evidence and which cannot:

1 Confirmational data – the client obtains 'the hard facts' (objective, direct and unambiguous) such as 'My wife has told me she's having an affair'.

2 Observational data – what the client has noticed which may point to a hard fact but the client could be making incorrect inferences like 'I saw my wife laughing while she was talking to a man in the high street and she was standing very close to him, so she must be having an affair with him'.

3 Conjectural data – stems from the client's hunches, impressions, intuition, 'I just know my wife is having an affair. You know what you know, do you know what I mean?'

Newman (1989) states that the level of evidence therapists ideally strive for is confirmational; however, what information is acceptable as evidence has to be agreed by both therapist and client if the therapeutic alliance is to remain productive. For example, a client's automatic thought was, 'People in my office treat me as if I'm stupid', and based her evidence on 'gut feelings', this being conjectural data from the therapist's viewpoint. Together, the therapist and client agreed to examine confirmational and observational data which constituted acceptable evidence. No one in the client's office had actually said to her face that she was stupid (lack of confirmational data), but the client presented lots of observational data to 'clinch' her case such as co-workers 'whispering and laughing and then looking in my direction', occasionally being the target of practical jokes and 'this person who talks to me in a kind of "do you understand what I'm saying?" voice as if I'm a moron'. In order to try and elicit confirmational data, the client agreed to confront the co-workers she thought were acting in a belittling or patronizing way towards her; this proved inconclusive as the general response was, 'What's your problem?' Her response to the automatic thought was: 'Some people at work are unfriendly towards me at times but I have no firm evidence that people think I'm stupid or treat me as if I'm stupid.'

The client suggested she might be overreacting to perceived slights because of her own insecurities about 'being a thicko' ('I left school as soon as I could. I suppose I do see myself as a thicko and believe that everyone else must think the same') and decided not to look 'for trouble' at work unless someone was acting offensively towards her (these insecurities became the focus of therapeutic intervention – if some people do think she is stupid, she cannot stop them from thinking it but she can learn to be clear in her own mind that she is not stupid). What confirmational data she could point to was that she was not part of the 'in-crowd' at work: 'They go nightclubbing a lot. I asked a couple of times if I could come along and they said "no".'

51

Constructing alternative explanations

This technique shows clients that there is more than one way of looking at a situation. Blackburn and Davidson suggest:

> Asking the patient to list alternative interpretations of a situation and then *establishing the realistic probability* of each interpretation is a powerful technique, as it does not reject the original negative interpretation, unlikely as it might be, and contrasts it with more likely interpretations.
>
> (Blackburn and Davidson, 1995: 76; emphasis in original)

In the following example, the client believes that the workshop she ran was a 'flop' because two evaluation forms out of twenty were critical:

Therapist: Okay, that's one view of the situation. What about the eighteen evaluation forms that were favourable?

Client: Well, I suppose it was reasonably successful then.

Therapist: Any other ways of looking at the situation?

Client: They felt sorry for me and that's why they gave me favourable feedback.

Therapist: How likely is it that they felt sorry for you?

Client: Highly unlikely. They were not a touchy-feely lot. They seemed quite hard to please in some ways.

Therapist: Any other explanations for getting favourable feedback?

Client: It was a fluke, a one off.

Therapist: It's hard to tell at this stage as it was your first workshop. Are you planning to do more? [client nods] Could there be other interpretations rather than it was a fluke?

Client: I gave a good performance.

Therapist: Anything else?

119

Client: They didn't have to pay to attend the workshop, so they scored me higher on the evaluation forms than they would have done if they were paying?

Therapist: Do you think they would put up with low standards just because they weren't paying? You did say they 'seemed quite hard to please in some ways'.

Client: I very much doubt they would have done that. I wouldn't if I was in the group.

Therapist: [writing on a whiteboard] So to sum up: your original thought about the workshop was that it was a 'flop' because two evaluation forms were critical. However, eighteen forms were favourable and in the light of this other explanations were: the workshop was reasonably successful, people felt sorry for you, it was a fluke, you gave a good performance and people didn't have to pay. Which explanation seems the most probable in the light of our discussion?

The client chose 'a good performance and I suppose that's why it was reasonably successful'; however, she still wondered if there were some 'fluky elements' involved in the success of the workshop and therefore suggested she run several more workshops over the next six months in order to collect data on her performance to resolve this issue: 'Do I have real skill or was the success of that first workshop sheer luck?'

52

Identifying cognitive distortions

In Point 2 we listed some common cognitive distortions such as all or nothing thinking and jumping to conclusions that are the results of faulty information processing when a person is emotionally distressed (for a full list see Leahy and Holland, 2000). The client can be given a list of cognitive distortions and asked by the therapist if he can identify the ones that are usually found in his thinking. (It is important that the therapist does not unintentionally indicate to her client that he may have *all* the distortions listed as he might believe he is truly 'cracking up'.) For example, a client with social anxiety said: 'I know that when I walk into a room people are thinking "he's boring, so I'll keep away from him" or if they do start talking to me then they quickly move away because they're thinking "he's so uninteresting".' The client quickly identified mind-reading as one of his key cognitive distortions, but then added: 'I believe I can read minds, it's true.' The therapist conducted an immediate experiment to test the client's ability to mind-read by writing the words 'Mickey Mouse' on a piece of paper; the client was unable to say what had been written down.

Mind-reading can be seen as a form of projection: 'The thoughts patients believe others are having about them are usually the very thoughts they are having about themselves' (Persons, 1989: 113). In the above example, if the client thinks he is boring, he is likely to conclude that others think in a similar way about him. The important point is for the client to read his own mind in a non-distorted way and stop attempting to read the minds of others (Neenan and Dryden, 2002a). These discussions (and experiment) with the therapist convinced the client that he was not a mind-reader: 'Realistically, I do not know what people think of me. I can ask them or go and talk to them to get some idea. Even if some people do find me boring that doesn't prove that I am, just that I can't please or interest everyone.'

Another key distortion of the client's was personalization which involves blaming oneself for causing a negative event without considering other factors. In the client's case, if a dinner party turned out to be dull he would conclude: 'It was my presence that put a dampener on things. If I hadn't been there, everyone would have had a great time.' The client was asked what other factors apart from his presence led to a dull dinner party. He produced the following list: interpersonal tensions among some of the dinner guests, a few guests wanted to hog the limelight all evening, some of the guests wanted to go home early, drunken 'loudmouthery', people wanting to sit somewhere else, the food was mediocre, just one of those evenings. The client could not have been responsible for other people's behaviour or how the dinner party turned out (it may have been dull to him but not to some or all of the guests): 'I may have made a contribution to producing a dull evening but there were lots of contributions I haven't considered. I certainly don't believe any longer that I'm responsible for what happened or that things would have been better if I hadn't been there.'

53

Looking at the advantages and disadvantages

This technique helps clients to tease out the advantages and disadvantages of adhering to a particular thought (e.g. 'Being on my own keeps me safe') or engaging in a specific behaviour (e.g. procrastination). Through discussion of each advantage and disadvantage, clients can learn to revise their self-defeating thoughts and change their counterproductive behaviours. Wells states that 'an effort should be made to generate more disadvantages than advantages . . . when the disadvantages of maintaining a behaviour or attitude outweigh the advantages, the individual should be more motivated to change' (1997: 72). The advantages and disadvantages of the above thought were written on the therapist's whiteboard:

Thought: 'Being on my own keeps me safe'

Advantages	Disadvantages
1 'I won't get rejected any more and feel terrible'	1 'And I won't have any more relationships to feel terrible about'
2 'I won't have anyone bossing me around'	2 'And I'll miss out on opportunities to learn to be more assertive in relationships'
3 'I can control my own life'	3 'And what an empty one it will be to control'
4 'I won't have to worry about becoming jealous and my emotions running riot'	4 'All I have to worry about is becoming an emotional desert'
	5 'My life is mapped out for me in all its bleak solitude'
	6 'Life without a relationship is not much of a life. I don't want that'

At the end of this exercise the thought had no further appeal to the client, but she wanted to learn to be more resilient in coping with the vicissitudes of relationships ('I can also be safe in a relationship if I learn to take the rough with the smooth and not see the end of a relationship as a great catastrophe'). For example, the client felt terrible when she was rejected because she suffered a double rejection: from her boyfriend, then herself ('I can't be any good if he's left me'). Part of developing a resilient outlook was for her to deal with the first rejection without creating a second, self-inflicted one ('He's rejected me but I'm not going to reject myself because of it'), understand that 'rejection' is a loaded term (i.e. charged with underlying self-denigratory meanings) and realize that relationships often 'fizzle out' rather than inevitably end in rejection.

Defining terms

This involves asking clients what they mean by the terms they use and thereby exposing any flaws in their thinking. For example, a client whose manuscript was rejected by a publisher stated: 'Because they didn't want it, this makes me a failure.'

Therapist: When you say you're a failure because the publisher rejected your manuscript, do you mean a failure as an author, man, person?

Client: As an author.

Therapist: How does rejection by a particular publisher make you a failure as an author?

Client: Well, it feels like it.

Therapist: Well, feelings are not facts. If you are genuinely a failure as an author then you had better not waste any more time on a hopeless cause. Now, when will all the evidence be in about whether you're a failure as an author?

Client: Some years from now, if not on my deathbed.

Therapist: So what would be an accurate description of your current situation?

Client: I've failed to impress one publisher with my manuscript but that doesn't mean I'm a failure as an author.

Therapist: What does it mean then?

Client: That I'm a struggling author who needs to keep on struggling if I hope to make my mark in the literary world.

Some clients might complain that defining terms is just semantic games (e.g. 'Change the words around and then I'll feel better, is that it?') but, in fact, it has a very serious purpose. Using words like 'failure', 'useless', 'worthless' or 'no good' to define oneself are not only dangerous overgeneralizations – a person might become depressed and consider suicide through such self-labelling – but are hopelessly inadequate and inaccurate in capturing the complexity and uniqueness of the self. Semantic precision helps clients to be clear and accurate about events (e.g. 'I've failed my driving test twice') and what can be done about them (e.g. 'I shall try for a third time') rather than focus on what they believe they are (e.g. 'I'm totally useless. I might as well give up now'), which will prevent them learning from their mistakes thereby restricting their self-development.

It is important that therapists do not become 'meaning maniacs', i.e. asking their clients what they mean by the terms that they use and then asking for the meaning of the new terms that the clients use to explain the old terms . . . and so on as this will develop into an infinite regress of meaning about meaning exhausting both therapist and client without reaching any helpful conclusions about which terms are meaningful in discussing problems (e.g. rating the specific behaviour or action is meaningful) and which are meaningless (e.g. rating the self is meaningless). Defining terms is a means towards an end of establishing semantic clarity; it is not an end in itself.

Reattribution

Reattribution helps clients to step back from and look at the many contributions to an adverse outcome. Thus, a client who blames herself for causing a bad outcome can be helped to see that she cannot be responsible for all the factors that led to this outcome. Self-blame for 'causing' negative outcomes is particularly evident in guilt and depression (Dattilio and Freeman, 1992). For example, a client said that she felt guilty because her 30-year-old son was 'not fulfilling his potential, just drifting through life and drinking heavily', and blamed herself for her son's difficulties ('I've failed him somewhere along the line. It's my fault he's like that'). This statement reflected the client's assumption of omnipotence, i.e. she has the power to control her son's destiny.

By listing as many factors as possible that have contributed to her son's difficulties (e.g. never keeping a job for long, being in debt, falling behind in his maintenance payments, heavy drinking, falling out with his neighbours, not caring about his appearance), the client realized eventually that her ability to influence, let alone control, her son's life was severely limited ('He doesn't pay any attention to me. He just accuses me of nagging him all the time which he gets angry about. At the end of the day, it's his life and he's responsible for it. I hope things improve for him'). Reattribution is not meant to let clients 'off the hook' but to help them assess accurately their level of responsibility in producing a particular outcome. In the above example, the client said, 'I'm probably not helping him with my nagging, so I've told him I'll be there for him whenever he asks for my help but I'm not going to pester him any more.'

Some clients blame external factors for 'causing' particular events, such as a client blaming work pressures and a demanding boss for 'making me start drinking heavily again'. With such clients 'the therapist can help individuals to reattribute responsibility for their drug use to themselves so that they may take initiatives to modify drug-using behaviors' (Beck *et al.*, 1993: 142). If the client can choose to use alcohol to deal with work pressures and a demanding boss, the client can also choose to find an alternative and more constructive way of dealing with these difficulties: 'I need a stress management programme more than alcohol to help me cope. My drinking is increasing the pressure on me, not reducing it.'

56

Decatastrophizing

This is taking the 'horror' (emotional disturbance) out of a feared event by encouraging clients to see themselves dealing with their catastrophic predictions. Catastrophic thinking is often generated by 'what if . . .?' statements such as 'What if I panic in the supermarket?' or 'What if I fail my exams?'(see Point 39). Barlow and Cerny state that 'the general strategy for decatastrophizing is to encourage the client to outline specifically the consequences of the feared event' (1988: 132). For each catastrophic consequence, the client can be helped to generate problem-solving alternatives:

'What if I panic in the supermarket?'

Consequences	Alternatives
'I'll make a complete fool of myself. People will laugh at me and think I'm pathetic.'	'I could be a coper instead of a fool and surprise myself. What people think and do I have no control over but I don't have to think I'm pathetic or laugh at myself. Having panic attacks is not a crime.'
'I'll never be able to go into that supermarket again as people will remember me and point me out.'	'The only person who is going to remember is me. I'm assuming that my panic attack is burned into people's memories. That's nonsense. People will only point me out if I walk around the supermarket naked!'

Beck *et al.* observe that 'when predicting dire consequences, the anxious patient does not utilize all of the information available to him and rarely takes into account his past dire predictions that failed to materialize' (1985: 208). This information includes rescue factors in the situation such as staff and some customers coming to the client's aid if she does have a panic attack in the supermarket; any embarrassment or humiliation she experiences will be time-limited, not suffered indefinitely; high levels of anxiety are bearable rather than unbearable and she has coped successfully with her panic attacks in other situations. Barlow and Craske (1989) suggest that decatastrophizing can be summed up in one phrase – so what? (i.e. the client can learn to accept and tolerate what she fears). However, these authors concede that the 'so what' strategy would be inappropriate with client fears of death or loss of significant others and that focusing on overestimation ('How likely is it that this feared outcome will actually occur?') is the more appropriate strategy in these cases. (Burns [1989] devotes a chapter in his book *The Feeling Good Handbook* to dealing with the fear of death.)

Newman suggests a creative challenge to negative 'what if . . .?' thinking by asking clients to give equal consideration to positive 'what if . . .?' thinking:

> Clients rarely if ever give equal time to the positive, literally *opposite* question, 'What if I succeed?' Therein lies a fundamental cognitive bias, because an objective assessment of future outcomes requires the careful consideration of both the positive and negative possibilities.
>
> (Newman, 2000: 140; emphasis in original)

Exploring double standards

Some clients apply a standard much more strictly to themselves than they do to others. For example, a mother condemned herself as bad when her child fell over and injured himself while out playing ('I can't be any good as a mother for letting this happen'), but has words of sympathy and understanding, not condemnation, for a friend whose child suffered a similar misfortune ('It can't be helped that children injure themselves when they're out playing. You can't keep them cooped up indoors all day, can you? You musn't blame yourself for what happened'). By eliciting the client's reasoning for this difference in her approach towards herself and her friend, the therapist can understand the basis for the client's double standards ('I have to be the perfect mother for my son to make up for not holding the marriage together. I just feel I've always got to be there for him, to protect him from harm, keep him safe'). Butler and Hope point out that a person with double standards based on valuing herself less than others continually undermines herself: 'It is like trying to build a house on top of a swamp. The house will not last, and its foundations will be constantly eroded' (1996: 17). The client can also be encouraged to explore the effect on her friend if she did condemn her ('Well, she'd be upset already over what happened and if I said she was no good as a mother that would make her feel worse').

The therapist can encourage his client to talk to herself in the same sympathetic way she would do to her neighbour in order to answer her NATS: 'It takes two, not one, to hold a marriage together. There is no such thing as a perfect mother, only a mother trying to do her best for her children. It's unrealistic to think I can always keep my son safe from harm. So as a mother, I'm good enough.' Through such self-discussion, double standards can be ditched and replaced with a single standard that is helpful, compassionate and realistic (Burns, 1989).

Modifying imagery

NATS come in visual as well as verbal form. Some clients find it easier to work with images rather than thoughts to achieve cognitive modification of their NATS. When clients visualize negative events, they often stop at the moment when their worst fear is being realized, as if the 'film' has broken down and they do not see what happens next. For example, a client had graphic images of seeing himself turn into a 'sweating, gibbering, nervous wreck rooted to the spot' when people laughed at him for spilling water over himself during a presentation. Wells suggests it is 'useful to "finish-out" images and take them beyond the worst point. This procedure reduces the amount of distress accompanying the image and shifts the patient out of danger processing mode' (1997: 76). The client is asked to restart the 'film':

Therapist: What's happening right now?

Client: They're still laughing at me. I'm blushing terribly. I'm tongue-tied and still rooted to the spot. I can't move.

Therapist: What about one minute later?

Client: I'm beginning to move about a bit and am beginning to nod my head and attempt to smile as if I'm in on the joke.

Therapist: Are they still laughing as much?

Client: No. The laughter is beginning to die down along with my blushing. I'm taking some deep breaths to get myself more under control. I'm smiling more now and pointing to myself saying 'clumsy fingers'.

Therapist: What's happening five minutes later?

Client: I'm continuing to give the presentation but I'm still feeling a little shaky and tongue-tied. I'm wondering what they think of me but I'm doing my best to focus on the presentation.

Therapist: And thirty minutes later?

Client: I'm much more in control now and feeling better. I prove this to myself by having a drink of water without spilling it. There are a few titters when I pick up the glass but after drinking it without spilling any, I stretch out my hand and say to the group 'much better now'. Then it's time for lunch which I feel much relieved by.

The client's imaginal journey through the worst and beyond demonstrates to him that he will not be stuck in that 'awful' moment for ever. The client practised this imagery exercise as a homework assignment and later declared: 'I don't think it would be a big deal any longer if it did happen to me. To be honest I'm getting bored with it. So what if I spill water over myself?' The general thrust of imagery modification in CT is to help clients change the negative direction of their imagery towards positive and more successful coping scenes (Dattilio and Freeman, 1992).

59

Behavioural experiments

These are used to test the validity of clients' automatic thoughts and intermediate beliefs (assumptions and rules). Behavioural experiments are used in the service of cognitive change. For example, a client who was very self-conscious about being overweight was unhappy about not 'allowing myself to go swimming'. If she went swimming her prediction was: 'People will stare at me and snigger and I won't be able to stay there' (the client said she wanted to stay in the pool for at least thirty minutes). The client anticipated that her level of anxiety would be 85 per cent in carrying out the experiment. The information collected from the experiment was discussed in the next session:

> *Therapist*: What actually happened in the swimming pool?
>
> *Client*: There were people there of all shapes and sizes, so that was a relief.
>
> *Therapist*: Okay, but what about your specific prediction, 'People will stare at me and snigger and I won't be able to stay there.' Did that prove true or false?
>
> *Client*: False. Obviously people looked at me – I was looking around too – but as far as I could tell no one was staring or sniggering at me. There was lots of shouting, laughing and people enjoying themselves.
>
> *Therapist*: How long did you stay in the pool for?
>
> *Client*: About an hour.
>
> *Therapist*: What about your anxiety level? You said that would be 85 per cent.
>
> *Client*: That came down to about 40 per cent. After about ten or fifteen minutes I was much less self-conscious and focused on my swimming rather than looking at others to see if they were looking at me.
>
> *Therapist*: So how would you respond to your prediction?
>
> *Client*: Obviously people did look at me but as far as I was aware no one sniggered at me and I was able to stay

there. However, I do need to go swimming at least once a week if I'm to feel less self-conscious in my swimming costume and see the trip as enjoyment rather than as an ordeal.

The therapist should not assume that just because a behavioural experiment has proved successful that an adaptive cognitive response has been generated. In evaluating the data from the experiment, the client may have concluded: 'If the pool had been less crowded then I would have stood out more. People would have stared and sniggered at me.' In this case, trips to the pool could be arranged when it was less crowded to test this prediction. Also, coping responses would be developed – not only to deal with any possible sniggering but also to stay in the pool and leave when she decided to rather than prematurely because she found the sniggering unbearable.

Socratic questioning (guided discovery)

As well as eliciting NATS (see Point 33), Socratic questioning is also employed to assist clients to 'open up' their thinking in order to develop alternative interpretations of problematic situations that better fit the facts. As Beck *et al.* observe:

> Questioning leads patients to generate options and solutions that they have not considered . . . [and] this approach puts patients in the "questioning mode" (as opposed to the "automatic impulse" mode) so that they will start to evaluate more objectively their various attitudes and beliefs.
>
> (Beck *et al.*, 1993: 29)

Also, through such questioning, clients are enabled to provide their own replies to their NATS rather than accept any interpretations that might be offered by the therapist. Padesky (1993b) suggests that Socratic questioning consists of four stages: (1) asking informational questions; (2) listening attentively and reflecting back; (3) summarizing newly acquired information; and (4) asking analytical or synthesizing questions to apply the new information to the client's original problem or thought. These four stages will now be demonstrated in the following dialogue:

Client: I'm worried about meeting some new people this weekend.
Therapist: Do you know what you're worried about?
Client: What they will think of me.
Therapist: What do you think they'll think of you?
Client: They'll think I'm a rather boring person and limit the time they spend with me. That's what I'm worried about. I'm not exactly the life and soul of the party type. I'm more of a quiet type. That's not a crime, is it?

[These questions have made the problem understandable to both therapist and client – Stage 1.]

Therapist: Hmm. In listening to you, it seems that you might think that being a quiet type is a crime. Is that true?

Client: I suppose it is: it shouldn't be a crime but some people like my boisterous work colleagues might think so. If you're quiet you must be boring. That would be their reasoning.

Therapist: [ponders] Does it have to be your reasoning as well? Is it others' opinions of you that make you boring or do you see yourself as intrinsically boring because you're quiet?

Client: I never thought of it like that. I suppose I do agree if others think I'm boring.

[The therapist's reflections have brought information into the client's awareness that was currently outside of it – Stage 2.]

Therapist: And if you didn't agree with others' opinions of you, but thought about this issue more carefully, then what?

Client: Well, I am a quiet person who is not to everyone's taste, but I don't see myself as intrinsically boring. I have interests, I read a lot. I'm reasonably happy with my life.

Therapist: So it seems that you can make up your own mind whether or not you consider yourself to be boring rather than agreeing with others' opinions of you. You said you have interests, read a lot and are reasonably happy with your life.

[The therapist summarizes the new information that has been revealed – Stage 3.]

Client: That's all true.

Therapist: So how does this information you have just supplied fit in with your original idea that you would agree with others if they thought you were boring?

[The therapist asks a synthesizing question to bring new information to bear on the client's original idea that he is boring if others consider him to be – Stage 4.]

Client: It doesn't fit in. I decide what I am.
Therapist: How will you remind yourself of that?
Client: By writing it down and going over it every day – 'Some people may think I'm boring but I see myself as an interesting person.'

Modelling Socratic questioning for clients helps them to observe and practise this skill as part of their developing role as a self-therapist.

Exaggeration and humour

This technique takes clients' self-defeating ideas to extreme conclusions in order to show them the inherent absurdity of these ideas and thereby generate more realistic ideas about the problematic situation. In this example, the client has made some accounting errors at work:

Client: I can't help thinking that something dreadful is going to happen because of my mistakes.

Therapist: [with mock seriousness] The company will close down, hundreds will be unemployed, whole industries will disappear overnight, the country will grind to a halt and a global recession will be unleashed.

Client: [laughing] You're laying it on a bit thick aren't you?

Therapist: You did say 'something dreadful is going to happen' because of your mistakes.

Client: Okay, I get the point. It's not dreadful then as that's going over the top, but my boss will probably haul me over the coals for the mistakes. That is realistic.

The use of exaggeration and humour 'may not be a good idea for the patient who is so extremely fragile and vulnerable that he feels ridiculed or criticized by the therapist's humorous or sarcastic remarks' (Persons, 1989: 136). The therapist should use these techniques only after a sound therapeutic relationship has been established with her client and emphasize to him that they are directed at his ideas, not him. Once these techniques have been used, feedback should be elicited from the client to determine their impact upon him.

62

Writing down alternative responses to NATS

We have indicated in Point 47 that the first three columns of the daily thought record (DTR) form are used for recording and distinguishing between situations, thoughts and feelings. The process of examining NATS leads to clients filling in column four with their alternative responses to these thoughts (see Appendix 2). These responses should be based on considering all the available evidence and not on the first unconsidered thoughts that pop into the client's mind – no automatic responses! – otherwise these responses may be unrealistic, overly positive or even more dysfunctional than the thoughts they are answering. To return to the example in Point 47, the client was angry (emotion) about her husband going off to play golf on a Sunday morning (situation). Her NATS were:

NATS	*Alternative responses*	*Outcome*
'He should want to be with me but as he doesn't, this means he's stopped loving me.' (80%)	'I'm mind reading again and jumping to conclusions – the wrong ones. He does want to be with me but not all of the time for heaven's sake!' (95%)	Angry (30%)
'Why the hell is golf more important than me?' (80%)	'Golf is important to him on a Sunday morning but it is not more important than me. He's told me that often enough. I need to be reassured over this issue which is my problem, not his.' (90%)	

continued

143

NATS	*Alternative responses*	*Outcome*
'I'm a golf widow and he doesn't give a damn.' (80%)	'A Sunday morning once a week does not make me a golf widow. If he didn't give a damn about my feelings he'd always be on the golf course or out somewhere else.' (90%)	

The client was asked to rate her belief in her alternative responses to her NATS and then re-rate the intensity of her anger (it was originally 85 per cent) in the light of these responses to determine if they had any positive impact on her mood. The client's comment – 'I need to be reassured over this issue' – may point to an intermediate belief (e.g. 'If he doesn't want to be with me all the time, then this proves he doesn't really want me') and/or core belief (e.g. 'I'm unlovable'), which would require examination and modification later in therapy. Filling out DTR forms helps clients to see that cognitive change leads to emotional change. As they gain more competence and confidence in completing these forms, the process of identifying and responding to NATS quickens thereby allowing clients to carry out this process mentally. The DTR forms can always remain on standby if clients need to 'return to basics' intermittently.

Homework

Rationale for homework

If a client spends one hour per week in therapy, he needs to be encouraged to devote some of the remaining 167 hours to carrying out homework tasks before his next appointment. Homework provides opportunities for clients to practise in everyday life the CT skills they have learned in the therapist's office. As Persons observes:

> No matter how many insights and changes occur during the session, patients will not solve the problems on their problem list or make significant changes in their underlying irrational beliefs unless they make behavioral and cognitive changes outside the session.
>
> (Persons, 1989: 141)

Clients often say they believe intellectually but not emotionally their adaptive responses to their negative thinking. This division between 'head and gut' thinking hinges on clients' degree of belief or conviction in these responses, such as when a client says: 'I know up here [tapping head] that I can be happy without a partner but I don't feel it down here [tapping stomach].' In order to test this 'gut truth', the client agrees not to look for a partner for several months and, instead, focus on activities that will help her to become more self-reliant. This assignment helps the client to strengthen her conviction that she can be happy living on her own (i.e. she believes it intellectually and feels it emotionally) and weaken her conviction that she cannot be happy without a partner. When she does decide to look for a partner it is now out of choice, not desperation or need.

Beck *et al.* state that 'the patient is encouraged to view homework as an *integral, vital component* of treatment. Homework is not just an elective, adjunct procedure' (1979: 272; emphasis in original). Therefore, clients are encouraged from the first session onwards to carry out homework tasks rather than delay the implementation of these tasks until they feel comfortable with the CT format. Homework tasks are agreed collaboratively, but in the early stages of CT the therapist usually takes a more active role in setting such tasks.

Homework allows clients to develop both competence and confidence in tackling their problems, thereby reducing not only the chances of a full-blown relapse but also the dangers of becoming dependent on the therapist for answers to their problems. The ultimate goal of CT is for clients to become their own therapist or problem-solver; homework facilitates and accelerates progress towards this goal and thereby reduces the time clients spend in therapy. Burns suggests 'that compliance with self-help assignments may be the most important predictor of therapeutic success' (1989: 545) and the therapist can point this out to those clients who are dragging their feet over executing such assignments. If clients object to the term 'homework', the therapist can ask them to use their own idiosyncratic usage.

Types of homework assignment

These assignments can be divided into two categories: cognitive (including imagery) and behavioural. Cognitive assignments include:

1 *Bibliotherapy*. These are reading assignments which not only help clients to understand their psychological disorders better but also the CT methods for tackling them. There is a substantial CT self-help literature from which selected titles can be recommended to clients such as *Love is Never Enough* by Aaron Beck (1988) for relationship problems, *The Feeling Good Handbook* by David Burns (1989) for dealing with depression and anxiety, *Overcoming Anxiety* by Helen Kennerley (1997), *Overcoming Low Self-Esteem* by Melanie Fennell (1999) and *Life Coaching: A Cognitive Behavioural Approach* by Michael Neenan and Windy Dryden (2002b) for developing greater personal effectiveness in one's life. Self-help literature is seen as an adjunct to therapy, not as a substitute for it.

2 *Listening*. Clients can be encouraged to tape-record each session in order for them to reflect upon its content away from the therapist's office; some clients may listen several times to each session to gain maximum therapeutic benefit from it. Clients often process information poorly during sessions because they are emotionally upset or they may be reluctant to admit they do not understand the points the therapist is making. On their own, they are less likely to feel inhibited or distracted and therefore more able to focus on the session tape. If clients do not want their sessions taped, then the therapist would comply with this request.

3 *Writing*. Filling out Daily Thought Record (DTR) forms or variations of them is a staple homework task. These forms help clients to record and respond to their upsetting thinking in more objective ways (see Points 47 and 62). Writing assignments can encompass any project that will benefit clients in tackling their problems, such as a client who agreed to write an essay entitled 'Is

endless people-pleasing the best way to develop self-acceptance?' and concluded at the end of it that people-pleasing was 'psychological servitude that I'm determined to get free of and focus more on being myself'. An action plan was then developed to translate determination into an achievable reality.

4 *Coping imagery*. This task helps clients to imagine themselves coping in situations where they fear an unpleasant outcome, e.g. a client who fears that 'I will be dumped after my first date if I'm not witty and good fun all evening' imagines himself carrying on a conversation without straining to be witty and good fun, and keeping an open mind as to how the evening will turn out.

5 *Inaction versus action imagery* (Neenan and Palmer, 1998). Clients who are unmotivated to engage in problem-solving thereby remaining stranded in problem-perpetuation are asked to imagine graphically the consequences of not dealing with their difficulties (e.g. endless procrastination, never going after what they want from life) and then contrasting this bleak picture with action imagery (e.g. taking risks to create interesting/exciting opportunities, doing instead of stewing). Clients are asked to carry out this exercise on a daily basis for the next few weeks while gradually fading out the inaction imagery and keeping an action log to determine if productive action is actually occurring.

Behavioural assignments include:

1 *Activity scheduling*. This technique is used frequently with depressed clients to increase their activity levels and reduce their indecisiveness and rumination on negative thoughts or experiences by structuring their days with a series of agreed activities. Each day is usually divided into hourly periods of planned activity so clients do not have to decide every hour what to do next. Clients are asked to rate on a 0–10 scale how much pleasure and sense of accomplishment they have gained from each activity. This rating scale helps clients to test their predictions that carrying out these activities will bring neither pleasure nor accomplishment.

2 *Graded task assignments*. These help clients to tackle their problems in small, manageable steps rather than attempting too much too soon. A hierarchy of feared or difficult situations can be drawn up with the client moving through the hierarchy at his own pace,

culminating in him facing the most difficult or feared situation. For example, a person with a dog phobia watched a dog playing from a safe distance, then began to move closer until he was able to stroke a tethered dog before facing his ultimate fear of an untethered dog 'sniffing' around him. He was able to overcome his fear within a few days.

3 *Experiments*. These enable clients to test their thoughts and beliefs, to treat them as hypotheses rather than as facts. For example, a client believed that his heterosexual friends would drop him if he told them he was gay. He said he wanted to 'stop living a lie and come out into the open'. His announcement of his sexual orientation provoked a range of reactions: 'we knew', disbelief, support, wariness among some male friends, and a few did 'drop me'. The client's prediction was, to a large extent, not realized and he felt relieved by the outcome; but some difficulties now emerged, such as 'some of my male friends are worried that I might fancy them'. How he would handle these difficulties received therapeutic attention. If all the client's heterosexual friends had dropped him, then the therapist would have helped him to examine the quality of his pre-disclosure relationships with them, find ways of accepting the grim reality of events and consider how he would approach forming future friendships with heterosexuals.

It is important for therapists to read the research literature on the efficacy of CT homework assignments and, based on what they have learnt from this undertaking, to develop a portfolio of effective between-session tasks for use with their clients.

65

Negotiating homework assignments

Obvious as it may seem, negotiation is based on collaboration, not telling the clients what assignments to carry out (telling may occur, for example, because the therapist wants her client 'to feel good about himself' as quickly as possible as his rapid improvement will reflect her clinical competence). Homework assignments should be based on the work undertaken in the current session and linked to the client's goals, e.g. preparing an activity schedule in the session, then the client implementing it as homework in order to raise his depressed mood. The homework task needs to be stated in clear and concrete terms (e.g. 'I will make three phone calls from home in the next week to enquire about college courses'), as well as when it will be done (e.g. 'On Monday, Wednesday and Friday mornings').

Anticipated obstacles to carrying out the assignment need to be identified (such as 'I might forget') and solutions developed ('I'll leave a note by the phone so I won't forget'). Clients can be given a copy of the completed homework form (see Appendix 3) in order to remind them of what they have agreed to do. Sufficient time (e.g. ten or fifteen minutes) should be left at the end of the session for homework negotiation; if this process is rushed, misunderstandings may occur, such as the client not having a clear understanding of what he is supposed to do as the assignment has been couched in vague terms. If an appropriate homework assignment has emerged earlier in the session it can be discussed then or nearer the end of the session.

Other considerations for the therapist to bear in mind are assessing whether the client has the skills to execute the assignment (e.g. the client wants to act assertively in a specific context but does not understand what assertive behaviour actually is; in-session rehearsal of assertive behaviour would be required) and does the task actually interest the client (e.g. the client may feel duty-bound to fill out DTR forms but an action assignment would be more stimulating for her). More experienced therapists may help clients to list several homework assignments from which they can choose the most interesting and relevant one (Padesky and Greenberger, 1995).

The therapist should point out to her clients that homework is based on a 'win–win' formula: this means that whatever happens with homework tasks, important information will be obtained (anything that happens inside or outside of therapy is grist to the cognitive therapy mill). Thus, if the client completes the assignment, how was this accomplished? If the client carried out a task other than the agreed one, what happened to alter the task? If the client did not attempt the task, what prevented him from carrying it out? Homework is based on *learning*, not success or failure. If the client does not carry out any homework tasks, then the learning from this is that he will maintain his problems instead of solving them.

During the early stages of therapy, starting homework in the session provides the fillip for clients to continue it outside of the session. As Beck observes: 'Patients often describe the hardest part of doing homework as the period *just before* they start it – that is, motivating themselves to get started' (1995: 256; emphasis in original). For example, I (MN) saw a client who was procrastinating over starting her dissertation for her university course. She agreed to start the dissertation in the session, blocks were identified ('I want to write a brilliant opening paragraph that will really impress my tutor') and tackled ('I'll start with an adequate opening paragraph, revise it when necessary, and leave the tutor to decide what he makes of it'). Writing assignments, imagery exercises or practising new behaviours can be initiated before the end of the session and any difficulties in carrying them out can be addressed.

As therapy progresses, the client should be suggesting homework assignments as part of her developing role as a self-therapist as this will encourage her to continue to devise and execute self-help assignments once formal therapy has ended. The client is less likely to do this if the therapist has played the major role in homework negotiation throughout the course of therapy.

66

Reviewing homework assignments

Reviewing homework is usually the first item on the session agenda. Overlooking homework review creates three problems:

> First, the patients usually begin to think that the homework is not important and, therefore, that treatment is something done to them rather than something they actively work on even in the absence of the therapist. Second, the therapists miss opportunities to correct mistakes such as the patients inadequately responding rationally to their automatic thoughts. Third, the therapists lose the chance to draw helpful lessons from the homework and to reinforce these lessons.
>
> (Beck *et al.*, 1993: 109)

Reviewing homework should be detailed, not cursory: what did the client actually do or not do, what lessons were learned and what conclusions can be drawn (e.g. 'I stayed in the supermarket even though I felt panicky. I can tolerate feeling very uncomfortable and my catastrophic predictions did not come true. If I can cope with the supermarket, then I cope with anything'). A common problem is homework non-compliance. Persons (1989) suggests three common obstacles impeding homework completion: perfectionism (e.g. 'If I can't do the task perfectly, then it's not worth bothering about'); fear of failure (e.g. 'If I fail at the task, this will prove how useless I am'); and the need to please others (e.g. 'I can't see the usefulness of the task the therapist has suggested but I'll say I'll try to do it because I don't want her to think badly of me').

Tackling these obstacles, respectively, can start with Hauck's assertion that 'it is more important to do than to do well . . . think of success rather as a slight bit of improvement over what you were able to do before' (1982: 47); pointing out that failing is a process while failure is the outcome, so a person can experience a number of failings at task completion but eventually succeed in carrying it out (Neenan and Dryden, 2002a), and that the person may fail to execute a particular task but it is demonstrably false to say the person is a failure or useless because of it; and encouraging the client to voice her true reactions to the homework assignment and suggest one herself that she would find genuinely helpful.

Difficulties in executing homework assignments can be predicted from the client's case conceptualization (see Point 30), e.g. a client who presents with procrastination problems is likely to put off carrying out his homework tasks. To forestall or reduce these anticipated difficulties the therapist and client can devise an anti-procrastination plan to facilitate homework completion, otherwise therapy may well get bogged down in discussing endlessly his homework non-compliance – 'I didn't do the homework again' – thereby prolonging his procrastination problems instead of overcoming them. If the client has difficulty with a particular assignment or shows a pattern of home-work non-compliance, then this becomes part of the session agenda; on some occasions, reviewing homework can take up the entire session. Padesky and Greenberger (1995) stress that the therapist should not see homework non-compliance as resistance to therapy but, instead, adopt a problem-solving outlook ('Let's see if we can find a way to overcome this difficulty'): trying to break down resistance can lead to power struggles or impasses in therapy while the latter strategy is likely to produce helpful gains for the client and the therapeutic alliance.

Therapists need to monitor their own reactions to homework non-compliance, such as feeling angry because the client is not 'taking therapy seriously' or feeling anxious because continuing non-compliance on the client's part will prove that the therapist is incompetent – 'I should have found a way to tackle this issue by now.' Through supervision and/or filling out a DTR form, the therapist can generate adaptive responses to his own automatic thoughts such as:

- 'It's better to probe for the reasons behind the client's non-compliance rather than attribute it to her not taking therapy seriously. I might find some useful material to work on', and
- 'I haven't found a way to tackle it at the present time but I'll keep on trying. My clinical competence is not dependent on whether a particular client does or does not carry out her homework.'

Such adaptive responses will help the therapist to regain his clinical focus on tackling the client's obstacles to carrying out her homework assignments.

Ways of identifying underlying assumptions and rules

67

Revealing 'if . . . then' statements

Identifying and examining underlying assumptions and rules (see Point 3) occurs when clients have gained some skill and confidence in applying the cognitive model to their problems by answering their situation-specific NATS and completing some homework assignments (working on NATS 'chips away' at underlying beliefs). To tackle these beliefs before this stage has been reached may result in clients feeling overwhelmed, threatened, distressed or resistant and lead to premature termination of therapy.

A key way to identify an underlying maladaptive assumption is for the therapist to be alert for client statements using an 'if . . . then' construction such as 'If I don't do as I'm told, then my partner will leave me' (assumptions can also be expressed in an 'unless . . . then' form such as 'Unless I'm always on top of things, then my life will become totally chaotic'). The terms of the assumption are set by the 'if/unless . . .'; the 'then . . .' inflicts its punishment if these terms are not met. Fennell points out that 'sometimes the "If . . ./unless . . . , then . . . " is not immediately obvious, but you will see it if you look carefully' (1999: 165). For example, a client says his motto is, 'Don't get close', but when deconstructed shows its 'if . . . then' origins: 'If I get close to people, then they will reject me'; another client says that his policy is 'to keep one step ahead of the game', which when translated into assumptive form is 'If I don't keep one step ahead of people by anticipating their actions, then I'll be used or exploited by them in some way.' Another way to elicit an 'if . . . then' assumption is to provide the 'if . . .' part of it:

Client: Why do I always massively overprepare for a presentation? Why can't I just do a reasonable amount of preparation?

Therapist: Let's find some answers to your questions. If I don't massively overprepare for a presentation . . .

Client: Then I'll feel I don't really know my subject, give a poor presentation and lose my credibility.

Therapist: If I just do a reasonable amount of preparation . . .
Client: Then I'll probably struggle with some of the questions and lose my credibility because I really don't know my subject. It's a credibility issue then. That's why I massively overprepare.

While we stress looking for maladaptive assumptions in an 'if/ unless . . . then' form they can be expressed in many different forms, such as 'I don't deserve any happiness in life because of what I did', 'My worth is dependent on what others think of me' and 'Other people's needs are more important than mine.'

68

Spotting 'musts' and 'shoulds'

These are imperative statements driving the client's behaviour, such as 'I must always perform perfectly' and 'I should never let my friends down.' These rules are maladaptive because they are rigid and do not allow for human fallibility. Must and should statements 'usually link up with a hidden "or else"' (Fennell, 1999: 166) which the therapist helps to make explicit by asking: 'Is there an "or else" attached to those statements?' With the above examples, the 'or else' is, respectively, 'I'll become a mediocrity' and 'They will desert me.' Clients can learn to spot the 'musts' and 'shoulds' in their thinking once these are brought to their attention:

Client: I shouldn't forget to phone my mother. I should phone her when I say I will. I feel guilty when I don't phone her.

Therapist: You did say you have a very demanding job as well as a family to look after. Do you make any allowances for that?

Client: No. That should not make any difference. I shouldn't forget to phone my mother.

Therapist: Are you aware that you've used the word 'should' four times in your last two sentences?

Client: What of it?

Therapist: The word 'should' can act like a slave driver dictating to you what you should and should not do. Does that strike any chords in you?

Client: [nodding] It's true I do drive myself pretty hard. My head is like a pressure cooker sometimes. I do use that word a lot.

Therapist: Would you like to keep a diary for the next week and see how many 'shoulds' you can spot in your thinking?

Client: Okay. That should be interesting [laughs].

The client's 'or else' statement attached to 'I should phone her [mother] when I say I will' was 'This will prove that I am an uncaring daughter.' If the client is receptive, the therapist can inject some humour into this process of spotting shoulds and musts by asking her client: 'Have you been engaging in some S and M in the last week?'

69

Discerning themes in clients' automatic thoughts

The therapist can review with her client his Daily Thought Records (DTRs) in a range of situations in order to help him become aware of a particular theme(s) that may be recurring in his thinking. For example, a sample of the client's thought records at home, work and in social situations are, respectively, 'Everything has to be just right', 'I need to ensure that my colleagues see me in the way I want to be seen' and 'I can't enjoy myself without the right people around me.' The therapist can ask him if he can recognize a theme running through these thoughts or whether he can infer a particular rule or assumption underpinning them:

Client: I'm not sure what you mean.

Therapist: In doing this exercise with other clients, themes of rejection, failure, approval have been identified.

Client: I'm still not sure.

Therapist: Well, in going over these thought forms there seems to be the need for control in your life. Is that the case?

Client: That's true. I like everything to be the way I want it.

Therapist: And if everything is not the way you want it . . .?

Client: Then I think my life is out of control, falling apart. [the client's assumption has been revealed]

70

Investigating marked mood variations

Fennell suggests that 'high mood often indicates that the terms of an assumption have been met, just as low mood signals its violation' (1989: 204). Clients can investigate their high moods as well as their low moods in order to uncover important information about their assumptions and rules. Beck *et al.* suggest that when a client feels particularly happy about an event 'questions about his thinking may lead to his base rules. Many of the dysfunctional formulas "pay off" for the patient when they appear to be working' (1979: 249). For example, a client said that she felt absolutely delighted that her boss had given her a 'well done' for bringing in an important project on time – 'I was floating on a cloud all day.' The therapist probed to discover the reasons behind the client's elated mood:

Client: It feels great, I feel great. My self-esteem went sky high. I like being praised. Who doesn't?

Therapist: What does it mean to you to receive praise?

Client: That I'm liked and considered a worthwhile person.

Therapist: What do you have to do or be in order to be liked and considered worth while?

Client: I have to do my best to please others.

Therapist: So would you say that you act in accordance with the following assumption: 'If I do my best to please others, then they will like me and consider me a worthwhile person'?

Client: That sounds right. My boss praised me, I felt good. What's wrong with that?

However, her high mood did not last for long as her boss was critical of her a few days later when she was late for a meeting: 'I felt destroyed when he criticized me.' The negative assumption, the flip side of the positive one, triggered the client's depressed mood: 'If I fail to please others, then they will condemn and reject me.' Clients can keep a diary to monitor these marked mood variations to help them elicit what assumptions and rules they subscribe to.

71

The downward arrow

This is a technique used to uncover underlying beliefs such as assumptions, rules and core beliefs (Burns, 1989, 1999). As Beck *et al.* observe:

> Many patients are unable to articulate these underlying beliefs until they have been asked to consider the personal *meaning* that their more manifest thoughts have for them. Therefore, when patients exhibit strong negative emotions that seem to be far more intense than their automatic thoughts alone would cause, therapists can ask patients to probe a bit deeper by asking successive variations of the question "What does that *mean* to you?"
>
> (Beck *et al.*, 1993: 140; emphases in original)

By pursuing the personal meaning of hot (emotionally charged) thoughts, the therapist helps the client to peel back layers of thought until an underlying belief is revealed. The downward arrow locates the cognitive source of this strong emotion. Unlike responding to automatic thoughts, each thought uncovered in the downward arrow is accepted as temporarily true until a belief is revealed. (If the thoughts were challenged as they appeared this would undermine the downward arrow technique as the client's attention would be directed elsewhere thereby leaving maladaptive underlying beliefs intact.) In the following example, a client is very anxious about going out with a new boyfriend and puts it down to the thought that 'He's bound not to fancy me':

Therapist: Let's assume he doesn't fancy you, then what?
↓
Client: I'm back on the shelf.
Therapist: And if you are back on the shelf, why would that be upsetting to you?
↓

169

Client: Isn't it obvious?

Therapist: I need to hear it from you rather than take a guess myself, so why would that be upsetting to you?

$$\downarrow$$

Client: Because no one wants me.

Therapist: And if that's true, what would that mean to you?

$$\downarrow$$

Client: That I'll always be alone, stuck on the shelf.

Therapist: To sum up then: do you believe that 'If no one wants me, then I'll always be alone, stuck on the shelf'?

Client: Yes, that's what I believe. [client's assumption is revealed and confirmed]

Beck points out that 'asking what a thought means *to* the patient often elicits an intermediate belief [assumption/rule]; asking what it means *about* the patient usually uncovers the core belief' (1995: 145; emphases in original). Uncovering core beliefs through the use of the downward arrow is demonstrated in Point 81.

72

Memories, family sayings, mottoes

Fennell observes that 'rules have their roots in experience. Sometimes people can trace them back to particular early memories, or to sayings that were current in the household where they grew up. Identifying these may help you to understand the policies you have adopted' (1999: 170). For example, a client remembered her parents telling her not to 'get above yourself' when 'I started to sing my own praises or feel good about myself'. The client said she still remembered her parents' injunction to this day which stopped her from taking pride in her achievements, or enjoying the praise of others, as this would mean 'I'm being conceited'. Another client who was unassertive in his relationships, at home as well as at work, said that when he spoke up as a child he was criticized, rejected or sometimes physically punished: 'I learned to keep quiet, keep my head down.' His assumption, derived from his experience, was: 'If I speak up, then something bad will happen to me.' While this assumption had been adaptive as a child by protecting him from parental punishment, it was now maladaptive as he did not speak up for himself in relationships or pursue what he really wanted to do in life. A third client said he had 'perfectionists as parents' who pushed their children to be the best at everything that they did: 'The family motto was "Always be first".' While following this motto had helped the client to achieve considerable success in life through relentless determination, the physical and psychological costs of such determination were also considerable.

Recognizing voices from the past also includes those of teachers, friends and relatives (Butler and Hope, 1996). For example, a client said that he felt guilty if he took time out from his busy life to enjoy himself: 'I should be able to relax, have a laugh from time to time. What's wrong with that?' However, 'having a laugh' had associations in his mind with idleness and wasted time. When the therapist asked him if these associations were echoes from the past, he said that a schoolteacher he had greatly respected had frequently told him that 'Idleness was only to be tolerated in the grave. Don't waste a moment of your life.' The client had absorbed this message which had resulted in his 'maximize-every-moment' lifestyle and feelings of guilt when time was being 'wasted'.

Revising assumptions and rules

73

Behavioural experiments

In this point and the following ones (74–80), ways of revising underlying assumptions and rules will be discussed. Assumptions are best tested with behavioural experiments (Padesky and Greenberger, 1995; Mooney and Padesky, 2000). The 'If . . .' part of the assumption can be put to the test in order to determine if the 'then . . .' part will be realized. For example, a client believed 'If I say what I want, then others will see me as selfish and reject me.' As an experiment, on a night out with her girlfriends, the client stated what film she wanted to see and where she wanted to eat afterwards. To her surprise, her friends agreed and asked her why she did not speak up more often. She spoke up on several more occasions to test further her assumption with, again, no adverse consequences (though her friends did not always go along with her wishes). The client's reformulated assumption was: 'If I say what I want, then others will see it as normal behaviour but not always agree to do what I want.'

Another client thought: 'If I speak up in a group, then I'll say something stupid and everyone will laugh at me.' The client was anxious about carrying out this experiment and wanted reassurance that nothing bad would happen, but the therapist pointed out that if the outcome was known before it had occurred then it was not an experiment. The client did speak up in the group and stumbled over her words, which elicited some titters from a few group members. The client concluded from the experiment that her assumption had been proved correct. However, the majority of group members did not laugh, stumbling over her words is not a mark of stupidity (unless the client believes that it is) but a sign of her nervousness, and what laughter there was can be dismissed as insensitive unless, again, the client sees it as further confirmation of her stupidity. Reviewing the outcome of a behavioural experiment needs to be carefully carried out to avoid either the client or therapist jumping to conclusions. After such a detailed discussion, the client decided on a new and self-helping alternative to her old dysfunctional assumption: 'When I speak up in groups, my focus will be on learning and self-acceptance, not seeing myself as stupid or paying attention to others' laughter if I get things wrong.' Fennell suggests that 'alternatives to dysfunctional assumptions can be written on flash-cards for patients to read repeatedly until acting in accordance with them becomes second nature' (1989: 207).

Not all assumptions can be tested with behavioural experiments such as 'If I'm bad in this life, then I will suffer in the afterlife'. How can the 'then . . .' part of the assumption be tested? With this assumption, the therapist would want to know what the client means by 'bad': deliberately acting badly or the usual transgressions of a fallible human being? Will the client experience ceaseless suffering or will it be time-limited – and what would be the scale of the suffering? Is the client's God compassionate or vengeful? Through such discussions, the therapist is attempting to help the client construct a balanced view of what awaits him in the afterlife rather than his fixation on fire and brimstone.

74

Disobeying the 'shoulds' and 'musts'

Rules of living are often expressed in rigid should and must statements such as 'I should never let anyone down' or 'I must always be strong and capable'. One way to modify these rules is by disobeying them to determine if the implicit and unpleasant 'or else' attached to the rule will be realized ('I must always be strong and capable or else I will be despised if I show weakness and indecisiveness'). For example, a client's rule was: 'I should put in consistently long hours at the office or else my colleagues will see me as a slacker and I'll lose their respect.' She agreed to vary her hours at the office and came in later on some days and went home earlier on other days. To her surprise, most of her colleagues complimented her on 'starting to look after yourself instead of overdoing it', and stated that they never had regarded her as a slacker and it would take something very serious to occur for them to lose their respect for her; a few colleagues commented that they did not know nor were they interested in how many hours she worked as they were too busy with their own work (which helped to correct the client's overestimation of how much attention was paid to her and how much respect she had).

Revising rigid rules means making them reasonable and flexible. The client's new rule was: 'I don't mind working long hours when it's necessary, but not in order to try and influence the way my colleagues see me. I'll leave it up to them to decide whether or not I have their respect. I want to do my best at work rather than have to keep on proving myself to my colleagues.' As well as reasonable and flexible, new rules are often lengthy and elaborate in stark contrast to the all-or-nothing quality of the old rules: 'This reflects the fact that they are based on an adult's ability to understand how the world works at a deeper level and to take account of variations in circumstances' (Fennell, 1999: 183). Such a lengthy new rule can prove mentally cumbersome and be one which the client might 'trip over' when trying to remember or rehearse it, so the therapist can suggest that the client construct a pithy version of it such as: 'Be myself, not prove myself, at work' (which the client eventually extended to other areas of her life where she believed she must not lose the respect of others).

75

Redrawing personal contracts

Assumptions and rules can be viewed as contracts that clients have drawn up with themselves (Blackburn and Davidson, 1995). For example, a client's contract was, 'If I help my friends, then they should help me'; however, the terms of the contract were often unfulfilled as some of her friends did not help her when she requested it which left her feeling bitterly disappointed by her friends' 'betrayal'. Burns pinpoints what is wrong with these contracts – they assume a natural reciprocity: 'Reciprocity is a transient and inherently unstable ideal that can only be approximated through continued effort. This involves mutual consensus, communication, compromise, and growth. It requires negotiation and hard work' (1999: 174). The above client did not understand this important point and assumed that her friends instinctively knew the terms of her contract, but the reality was that the contract was unilateral, not bilateral; therefore it was invalid.

In order to stop feeling bitterly disappointed when some of her friends let her down, the client decided to rewrite her personal contract in more reasonable and realistic terms: 'When I help my friends, which I like to do, I will no longer automatically expect them to help me in return though it would be nice if they helped me sometimes.' Another client, who had recently lost his job, believed passionately in his unilateral contract, 'As I desperately want another job, then I should be given one'; unfortunately, each job interview failed to gain him one and he started despairing at the 'unfairness of it all'. The client was overlooking a simple fact: job applicants are picked for their skills and talents pertaining to the job, not on the basis of their desperation for one. The client rewrote his contract to reflect this fact: 'I very much want a job but no one has to give me one. I will keep on applying and making sure that my skills are appropriate for the jobs I go for. Every time I don't get the job I will ask for feedback to help me improve my interview skills.' The client was eventually successful at his eleventh job interview.

76

Examining the short- and long-term usefulness of assumptions and rules

Clients often focus on the immediate benefits to be derived from subscribing to a particular assumption or rule and are reluctant to look at its longer-term harmful effects; after all, why should they bother looking ahead when their assumptions or rules are currently producing good results for them? Beck *et al.* state that this is precisely the time to examine these assumptions and rules:

> Many who believe that they need the approval of everyone are often extremely happy when they think they have this approval. Others who believe their value depends on their performance are often overjoyed when they are performing well. The job of the therapist is to help the patient see the *long-term effects* of operating under these rules.
>
> (Beck *et al.*, 1979: 270; emphasis in original)

Clients who believe they need the approval of others in order to feel good about themselves are putting control over their feelings into others' hands (whether these others realize it or not): approval puts their mood up and disapproval brings it down. It is important for 'approval-seekers' to look ahead in order to see the emotional distress they are likely to experience when approval is withdrawn and to *immediately* start constructing more helpful assumptions and rules that do not make their self-worth conditional, such as: 'It's very nice to have people's approval, but it's not essential and it's unlikely to last. Better to develop self-acceptance which means I don't have to look to others in order to feel good about myself. Self-acceptance can be a constant factor in my life, approval from others usually isn't.' Those clients who link self-value to a particular performance can break this link by seeing the self as unrateable, only the performance is rateable: 'Whether my performance is good, bad or indifferent has no bearing on me as a person. I will learn to focus on evaluating the particular performance, not evaluating myself on the basis of it.'

77

Developing an alternative assumption that retains the advantages of the maladaptive assumption and jettisons its disadvantages

Maladaptive assumptions are often constructed in rigid and extreme terms such as 'If I don't always maintain my high standards, then this will prove I'm incompetent.' The client never felt any real enjoyment when he did maintain his standards because he was always worried about falling below them and became depressed when he did. The client acknowledged the need to modify this assumption but feared that in so doing his high standards would drop sharply: 'I know it sounds strange, but it motivates me to think that way and it's given me quite a bit of success':

Therapist: Your modified assumption would aim to keep the success and motivation but give up the self-downing and thereby avoid experiencing the depression that flows from it.

Client: It sounds good put like that but how do I actually change it?

Therapist: Well, look at the 'If . . .' part of your assumption, what's the troublesome word there?

Client: 'Always'. There's no leeway for allowing myself to fall myself below my standards because I do sometimes.

Therapist: And no compassion or understanding when you do. Look at the 'then . . .' part of your assumption.

Client: I worry that if I drop the 'always', then my standards will collapse.

Therapist: You've just stated another assumption and you need to put that to the test as well. You're investing the word 'always' with an almost mystical power. It has no power independently of you. You can deprive it of power if you stop believing in it and think of a non-extreme alternative that will lead to a different and compassionate conclusion when you fall below your standards. What sounds like a reasonable alternative to you?

Client: Okay. I really do want to maintain my high standards but . . . hmm.

Therapist: That's a start.

After further discussion with the therapist, the client's new assumption, which kept the 'good' parts of the old assumption and ditched the 'bad' parts, was: 'I really do want to maintain my high standards but when I fall below them, as I have done already, I will not condemn myself as incompetent. Instead, I will accept what has happened and see what I can do to put it right.' Obviously, verbalizing a new assumption in the therapist's office carries little conviction unless the client repeatedly and forcefully acts in support of it in a variety of situations where the old maladaptive assumption was operative. By the end of therapy, the client had experienced several occasions where he fell below his high standards (they did not collapse) and focused on 'what went wrong' instead of self-condemnation. He said that the time he previously wasted 'on feeling bad and putting myself down' was now channelled into productive problem-solving.

78

Listing the advantages and disadvantages of a rule or assumption

Clients can be encouraged to list and examine the advantages and disadvantages of holding a particular rule or assumption (see Point 53 for using this technique with automatic thoughts). In the following example, the client's assumption was written on the whiteboard in the therapist's office and the board was divided into two columns:

Assumption: 'If I'm not in control of my feelings, then I'll become unstable and hysterical'

Advantages	*Disadvantages*
1 'It keeps me emotionally strong'	1 'I feel emotionally repressed as well'
2 'People admire my sangfroid'	2 'It's often an act I put on for people because I'm scared of revealing how I really feel'
3 'To be honest, I feel superior to those who are an emotional mess'	3 'Feelings of superiority don't last for long. I begin to wonder who really is the emotional mess – them or me?'
	4 'Other people can express their feelings without becoming unstable and hysterical. I'm not giving myself the chance to experiment with my feelings'
	5 'I sometimes don't even allow myself to laugh too much in case people think I'm getting hysterical'

As usually happens with this technique, the disadvantages eventually outweigh the advantages (though the therapist may need to prompt clients to focus on the disadvantages as they more readily list the advantages than the drawbacks of their rules and assumptions). Clients can also be asked to re-examine the advantages in order to determine how advantageous they really are:

Therapist: Do you actually feel emotionally strong?

Client: Not really. A friend of mine can laugh or cry when the mood takes him. He's not worried what others think of him. That's true strength. I'm always worried what others would think of me if I was spontaneous with my feelings. I'm trying to control them all the time. I'm the real emotional mess.

Therapist: It doesn't have to stay that way.

With the disadvantages outweighing the advantages and some of the advantages revealed as self-defeating, clients are then likely to initiate change and thereby generate more functional assumptions, such as in the above example: 'I would like to experiment with my feelings rather than always holding back, pretending to be in control. I don't believe any longer that expressing my feelings, when it is appropriate, will lead to instability or hysteria but, instead, lead to a richer emotional life that I have denied myself for so long.' The client can now, with this assumption, explore new possibilities for himself.

79

Exploring the historical development of assumptions and rules

Fennell suggests that 'understanding how dysfunctional assumptions were formed promotes distance from them' (1989: 206) and thereby a more dispassionate evaluation of them can be conducted. This development usually starts early in life (but not inevitably so) as children form their assumptions and rules in the light of their experiences and relationships with others; these assumptions and rules help them to make sense of the world around them. For example, a child who is harshly criticized by her parents when she is naughty – 'You're a little devil. No one will ever like you if you don't behave yourself' – does her best to 'be good' thereafter. 'Be good' eventually becomes an unarticulated assumption: 'Unless I please others, they'll criticize me and then reject me as unlikeable.' While this 'be good' strategy may have been adaptive for the child in order to avoid parental anger and criticism, as an adult it has become maladaptive as the client is submissive in her relationships (home, work and social) and 'lives' too much in the minds of others ('I'm always wondering what people think of me. Do they like me? Have I upset them in some way? It's ridiculous but I can't seem to stop doing it').

By comparing and contrasting the operation of the assumption in childhood and adulthood, the client came to the conclusion that it had outlived its usefulness ('It's exhausting trying to please others and worrying about whether they like me or not') and led her to developing a moderate and self-helping assumption: 'I still want to please others at times but not because I feel I have to. I will start pleasing myself and speaking up for me. If I get criticized or rejected for it, too bad. I am likeable despite what others might think.' As always, a new rule or assumption is only theoretical when voiced in the therapist's office, so if it is to be internalized it needs to be put into daily practice in the client's life.

The client discovered that she greatly overestimated being criticized by others when she stood up for herself, and what criticism she did encounter enabled her to test the strength of her belief that she was indeed likeable despite what some people might think of her ('I don't get all sort of crumbly and wobbly inside like I used to when I thought someone didn't like me'). One of the most pleasurable changes she described was 'moving out of the minds of others and spending much more time in my own mind enjoying my own interests'. As dysfunctional rules and assumptions are usually long-standing, Fennell cautions that 'it could take as much as six to eight months for your new rule to take over completely. As long as the new rule is useful to you and you can see it taking you in useful and interesting directions, don't give up' (1999: 187).

80

Using imagery to modify assumptions

In Point 58 we looked at using imagery to modify NATS. Here we look at using imagery to revise dysfunctional assumptions. For example, an anxious client who has distressing images of fainting in the high street and being laughed at never gets imaginally beyond the 'fainting and the laughter'. Her assumption is: 'If I faint in public, then people will laugh at me and call me a drunk.' The therapist guides the client beyond the 'fainting and the laughter' to arrive at a different interpretation of the situation:

Therapist: Close your eyes and imagine you have fainted in the high street. What's happening now?

Client: I'm unconscious. People are pointing and laughing at me and saying 'She's a drunk.'

Therapist: How will you know what people are doing or saying if you're unconscious?

Client: That's true. I never thought of that.

Therapist: How long do you think you will be unconscious for?

Client: Only a couple of minutes.

Therapist: What do you see when you open your eyes? Anyone laughing?

Client: No. They're asking me if I'm okay and shall they call an ambulance.

Therapist: Can you hear anyone calling you a 'drunk' or anything else?

Client: I can't hear that. People are concerned for my welfare, helping me to my feet and picking up my handbag for me.

Therapist: What happens then?

Client: People say goodbye, I thank them for helping me and then they go about their business which my fainting interrupted. I walk home, a little bit unsteady on my feet but I feel okay by the time I get home.

Therapist: How are you feeling now about fainting in public?
Client: Much less worried.
Therapist: What's changed for you then?
Client: Well, if I faint in the high street, then people are much more likely to help me than laugh at me or call me a 'drunk'. It does seem a more realistic picture of how people will react. [client opens her eyes]
Therapist: Have you ever seen anyone faint?
Client: Yes I have. I saw someone faint in the shopping centre a few years ago and lots of people went to his aid. I don't know why I think people will be nasty to me. Do you know?
Therapist: We can discuss that later [client nods]. With this imagery exercise, you'll need to practise it regularly in order to strengthen in your mind this realistic outcome.
Client: I can see the sense in that.

This time projection exercise (Lazarus, 1984) enabled the client to construct a new assumption based on a realistic appraisal of the likely reaction of others to her predicament which was reinforced by her own recollections of public reaction to a person who had fainted. If the client had wanted to include in the imagery exercise someone calling her a 'drunk', the therapist could have asked her: 'Who has accurate knowledge about you: you or a complete stranger?'

Uncovering core beliefs

81

The downward arrow

When NATS have been answered, and dysfunctional rules and assumptions modified, core beliefs become the next target of therapeutic intervention (if this is clinically justified – see Point 16). Core beliefs are fundamental appraisals we make of ourselves (e.g. 'I'm not good enough'), others (e.g. 'You can't trust anyone') and the world (e.g. 'Everything is against me'). These are examples of maladaptive core beliefs – rigid and overgeneralized – which cognitive therapists help their clients to uncover. In this and the following points, (82–84), ways of uncovering core beliefs are demonstrated. The downward arrow (demonstrated in Point 71 to reveal a client's underlying assumption) pursues the personal meaning for the client of each thought elicited until a core belief is discovered. It is important that the therapist does not engage in challenging the client's thoughts as this will prevent the 'arrow' from going 'down' very far. Nor should she ask long-winded questions that will distract the client from the often intense introspective focus required of him for the successful completion of this exercise, or insert her own interpretations of the client's problems into her questions (such as: 'It seems to me that what you're *really* saying is that you're not a successful person. What does it mean to you to be an unsuccessful person?') In the following example, the client is very worried about her husband's sudden willingness to stay late at work:

Therapist: What's anxiety-provoking for you about that?
↓

Client: He might be having an affair.
Therapist: And if he is having an affair, what then?
↓

Client: Well he's going to run off with the bitch.
Therapist: And if he does run off with the 'bitch' . . . ?
↓

Client: [becoming tearful] I'll be all alone, unwanted.

Therapist: What does that mean about you if you are all alone, unwanted.

↓

[Asking clients 'What does that mean about you?' rather than 'to you?' usually reveals a core belief – see Point 71.]

Client: That I'm unattractive, repulsive. [core belief]

In the above example the client was 'very worried' about her husband's behaviour. As Padesky observes: 'Questioning the meaning of high affect [emotion] events will usually quickly lead to the identification of schemas [core beliefs]' (1994: 269).

Conjunctive phrasing

This refers to the therapist's use of phrases such as 'and that would mean . . .', 'and if that were true . . .' or 'and then . . .' to 'nudge along' her client's train of thought to its cognitive destination (i.e. core belief) by inviting him to finish his thoughts (DiGiuseppe, 1991b). The therapist removes the full stop at the end of the client's sentence and replaces it with a conjunction as in the following example:

Client: I might mess up things badly on my first date.
Therapist: If that were true . . . ?
Client: It would be a disaster.
Therapist: And that would mean . . . ?
Client: That I'm a total fuck-up. [core belief]

DiGiuseppe observes that an 'advantage of this method is that it keeps clients focused on their thoughts. The less a therapist says, the less clients have to respond to the therapist's words or attend to whether the therapist has understood them. The conjunctive phrase focuses clients on the meaning of their statements' (1991b: 168). We have used the term 'verbal economy' to convey the same point as DiGiuseppe's (Neenan and Dryden, 2000). Verbal economy should also be the guiding principle when carrying out the downward arrow technique (see previous point).

In the above example, the client's core belief was a "total fuck-up". It is important that the client's idiosyncratic usage is retained and not 'tampered' with by the therapist to protect her own sensitivities or in assuming that she is doing it for his benefit in order to moderate his emotional distress: 'When you say a "total fuck-up", which is a very harsh thing to say about yourself, do you mean that you see yourself as inadequate sometimes?' Discussing the development and maintenance of a maladaptive core belief and developing an alternative, adaptive core belief is more likely to be meaningful for the client when it is done within his frame of reference, not the therapist's. Sometimes a client's idiosyncratic usage needs investigating in order to tease out the core belief embedded within it, e.g. 'dipstick' means 'I'm stupid', and 'I'm an underwhelming kind of guy' translates as 'I'm boring'.

Sentence completion

As core beliefs are often stated in global terms, the therapist can write on his whiteboard or a piece of paper the following incomplete sentences and ask the client to 'fill in the blanks' in order to identify her core beliefs about herself, others and the world:

- I am . . . powerless
- People are . . . threatening
- The world is . . . dangerous

Another example of sentence completion would be for the client to reveal a core belief aided by the therapist's prompting:

> *Client*: I'm scared shitless about the workshop going horribly wrong.
>
> *Therapist*: You're scared shitless about the workshop going horribly wrong because . . . ?
>
> *Client*: That will prove I'm useless. [core belief]

Sentence completion just falls short of directly asking the client what her core beliefs are. Asking the client is the most straightforward way of eliciting core beliefs and should not be overlooked because the therapist favours more sophisticated techniques like the downward arrow to display his clinical skill.

84

Core beliefs appearing as automatic thoughts

As we have said in earlier points, situation-specific automatic thoughts are usually the first target of therapeutic intervention in cognitive therapy as they are the easiest level of thought to modify in order to bring symptomatic relief to clients. However, the therapist may run into trouble in attempting to modify a particular automatic thought because she is actually struggling with a core belief, not an automatic thought. Maybe the therapist's lack of knowledge or experience has contributed to this oversight or she believes that the client will automatically know what automatic thoughts are when she has explained them to him! In the following example, the client's core belief is 'hidden' in her outpouring of automatic thoughts but is detected by the therapist:

Therapist: What thoughts were going through your mind when you were told by your boss you were being made redundant?

Client: Bloody hell! Not again. You work your backside off and this is how things turn out. I deserve better than this. The boss was very impersonal about it; basically, clear your desk and then you're out. Wham-bam thank you ma'am. How am I supposed to pay the mortgage? Struggle, struggle, struggle, that's all I seem to do. 'Why bother?' I ask myself. I'm a failure [core belief], that's the reason. The whole process starts again. Trudging around for another job, more soul-destroying interviews. I know, who said life was easy. I just wish it was sometimes. I don't know . . . things just seem to keep going wrong for me.

Therapist: Sounds like pretty bad times for you, but before we look at these issues in greater depth can I bring your attention to something you said – 'I'm a failure'. Is this a central view you have of yourself or is it related to your current job difficulties?

199

Client: I'm not sure really. When times are bad I suppose I do see myself as a failure but when things are okay, I see myself as okay, normal. That's it really.

Therapist: Would you want to focus now on the 'I'm a failure' belief or leave it to later in therapy?

Client: No, leave it to later. It's losing my job and having to find another one I want to talk about. That's the major hassle in my life at the moment.

When a core belief is revealed at the stage of identifying automatic thoughts, the therapist wants to ascertain if the client realizes she has revealed a core belief and knows of its presumed importance in maintaining her emotional problems; and if she does realize its importance, is she ready, willing and able to work on it now or does she want to postpone schema (core belief) work until she has acquired some CT skills by working on her surface thoughts first. Generally speaking, schema work is usually carried out later rather than earlier in cognitive therapy because 'it is thought that challenging a patient's cherished beliefs too early in therapy will be counter-productive as the patient may feel threatened and resist change' (Blackburn and Davidson, 1995: 82). However, with clients who have personality disorders, the identification and modification of long-standing rigid core beliefs (e.g. 'I'm bad') starts early in therapy as these beliefs are activated in a wide range of situations and are the near-permanent outlook of such clients. As Davidson says: 'Core beliefs are the automatic thoughts in personality disorder' (2000: 31).

Developing and strengthening new/existing core beliefs

85

Educating clients about core beliefs

Educating clients about core beliefs (or schemas) serves as a prelude to modifying them. Core beliefs are usually formed in the light of early learning experiences. They can be both positive (e.g. 'I'm likeable') and negative ('I'm unlikeable'); most people have both. Core beliefs process incoming information and thereby determine how we perceive events; in a sense, we can only see what the core belief allows us to. Dormant negative core beliefs are often activated and thereby pass into our awareness at times of emotional distress, such as a client who becomes depressed following the end of his marriage as he believes 'I'm worthless without her'. With this belief dominant in his thinking, any information or experience that contradicts his schema is likely to be dismissed, distorted or overlooked; the client will more actively process information that confirms this belief. For example, the client is reluctant to accept any reassurances from his friends that he is still valued by them as this discrepant information would not 'fit' with his view of himself as worthless but, instead, focuses on information that would 'fit' with it: 'If I'm still valued so much by them, why are they coming round to see me less and less since my wife left me? They are lying.'

Core beliefs are perpetuated in three main ways: the schema processes of maintenance, avoidance and compensation (Young, 2002).

1 *Schema maintenance.* This refers to ways of thinking and behaving that maintain core beliefs such as a client who believes that she is inferior and therefore always puts others' interests and needs before her own. The client acts in accordance with the schema.
2 *Schema avoidance.* This refers to the cognitive, behavioural and emotional strategies that a client uses to avoid activating his core belief and the intense emotional distress associated with it, e.g. a client who refuses an invitation to a party because he believes he is unattractive to women and will feel 'devastated' going home alone,

tries to cheer himself up at home with wine and music ('I'll have my own party') but through his avoidance he reinforces his belief in his unattractiveness.

3 *Schema compensation*. This refers to thoughts and behaviours that serve to 'fight' against or overcompensate for a negative core belief. For example, a client who sees himself as unlikeable tries to convince himself that he is likeable by 'collecting' as many friends as possible ('An unlikeable person would not have this many friends'). However, as these friendships are superficial and transient the client finds it an uphill struggle to keep finding new friends which confirms for him that he is unlikeable ('If I was truly likeable I wouldn't have to work this hard to find and keep friends').

Clients may exhibit all three schema processes, but with some more prominent than others. Core belief education does not have to be detailed or drawn-out, e.g. a client who sees herself as stupid is told by the therapist (with examples to illustrate his point) that she repeatedly thinks and acts in ways that confirm her 'stupidity'; in order to stop confirming this belief, she needs to think and act in support of a new, positive core belief yet to be developed (which would be the next step): 'That's easy to understand but will it be easy to change my belief?' The therapist replies, 'It will require some hard work and risk-taking but changed it can be.'

Developing alternative core beliefs

As soon as clients' key core beliefs have been identified and schema education has begun, it is important for the client to start developing new and more adaptive core beliefs. Mooney and Padesky (2000) advise that these new beliefs should be stated in the client's own words, they do not have to be the thematic opposite of the old core belief (e.g. 'I'm incompetent' vs. 'I'm competent' or 'I'm useless' vs. 'I'm useful'), and that the main focus of clinical attention is on constructing and strengthening new beliefs rather than on modifying old maladaptive beliefs. Some therapists might believe that subjecting a dysfunctional core belief to empirical scrutiny will naturally undermine it and the client will then be free of its disturbance-producing 'grip' upon him. However, as DiGiuseppe points out, challenging dysfunctional beliefs is not sufficient to change them:

> People frequently hold on to beliefs that they know are logically flawed and do not lead to accurate predictions of reality, but no alternative ideas are available to replace the flawed idea. The history of science is filled with such examples. People do not give up ideas, regardless of the evidence against the idea, unless they have an alternative idea to replace it.
>
> (DiGiuseppe, 1991a: 181)

Therefore, the therapist should encourage her clients to focus on how they would like to be rather than let them linger on how they are. This focus can be initiated by asking clients something like this:

Therapist: How would you like to see yourself instead of as a 'failure'?
Client: I'm not sure.
Therapist: Let's think about it now. We don't want to spend the rest of therapy talking about you as a failure.
Client: I don't want that either. I suppose I would just like to see myself as reasonably competent.

Therapist: And what might your life look like if you were 'reasonably competent'?

Client: Well, I'd learn to take the rough with the smooth in life and not give myself a hard time when things go wrong. I'd like to be able to praise myself when I do things right. I don't know what else to say.

Therapist: That's fine. That sounds like a good start.

The therapist should not expect a client's new core belief to be fully formed and robust at the outset of schema work: the client's degree of conviction in his new belief will be gradually strengthened through the collection of evidence that supports it while his degree of conviction in his old belief will be weakened through the re-examination of evidence that used to sustain it.

Core belief work can be relatively straightforward or more difficult. In the former category, the client does have an existing positive core belief ('I'm pretty likeable') but this is difficult to gain access to currently because of his low mood following a falling-out with his best friend ('I just feel that no one likes me now. We've been friends since childhood'). Padesky (1994) suggests that producing contradictory evidence ('Let's make a list of the people you still are friends with') can quickly reactivate the client's positive belief and ameliorate his low mood within a few sessions of therapy. In the latter category, if a positive core belief is not present to which the therapist can appeal because of the client's long-standing problems which have interfered with the development of such a belief (the client has always seen himself as 'bad'), then the first step is to identify a positive belief, even if this is difficult to do given the client's disturbed state, for 'without an explicit alternative (even if it is only initially minimally believed, and that on an intellectual rather than emotional level), the patient has nowhere to "store" information contrary to their current negative belief' (Fennell, 1997: 14).

87

Use of a continuum

Clients' negative core beliefs are often constructed in all or nothing terms such as, 'You're either a success or failure in life and I'm one of life's failures'. The use of a continuum (i.e. a scale from 0 per cent to 100 per cent) introduces shades of grey into clients' thinking thereby helping them to develop more balanced and realistic appraisals of themselves, others and the world (to arrive eventually at the mid-point on the continuum). Padesky and Greenberger suggest that 'a scale or continuum is most therapeutic when it is constructed and its data evaluated for the new schema rather than the old. A small shift that strengthens the new schema is usually more hopeful for the client than a small shift that weakens the old schema' (1995: 144).

For example, if schema change is evaluated along a continuum focusing on the old belief ('I'm worthless'), the client might declare that 'I'm only 80 per cent worthless now' and see therapy as helping him to reduce his sense of worthlessness, whereas if it is evaluated along a continuum based on his new belief ('I'm okay as a person') optimism can be engendered that his new view of himself is gaining ground ('It has increased from 15 to 20 per cent since I last saw you'). When the continuum is being constructed, the therapist should help her client to define the end-points on the continuum in extreme terms so that he can see more clearly that change is occurring (if there is not a very strong contrast between these end-points, this will limit the client's perception of how much change he is achieving). In the following example, the 0 per cent, 50 per cent and 100 per cent points on the continuum are defined by the client:

New core belief: I'm reasonably competent

0%	50%	100%
Never competent	Competent and sometimes incompetent	Always competent

The client is asked where he would currently put a cross on the continuum ('At 10 per cent'). The continuum can be a regular reference point to monitor clients' progress towards the mid-point based on information and evidence collected from various sources such as positive data logs (see next point). A few clients may want to get to the 100 per cent point eventually but this will mean that what starts out as an adaptive belief is gradually transmuted into a maladaptive one (as it is highly unlikely the client will always be competent). The continuum is designed to help clients develop a rounded view of themselves and their experiences.

88

Positive data logs

These logs help the client to collect information over the coming weeks and months to support her new adaptive belief and counteract her tendency to focus only on information that confirms her maladaptive beliefs; in other words, to correct her faulty information processing. A major difficulty in collecting positive information is the reflex of the old core belief to discredit or discount any information that contradicts it. Padesky (1994) likens this habitual response to holding a prejudice against oneself or others (Flew states that a prejudice refers to beliefs 'which are either formed prior to proper consideration of the evidence or held in defiance of it' [1975: 29]). For example, a client's new core belief is 'I am attractive to some women' but when a woman seems interested in him at a party his old belief, 'I'm unattractive to women', discounts this: 'She's only passing the time with me until she sees someone she really does fancy.' The client becomes despondent that the old belief is the 'real truth about me and I'm deluding myself in trying to believe anything different':

Therapist:	What happened with that woman who seemed interested in you?
Client:	She went off to chat to someone else. The story of my life.
Therapist:	Why do think she chatted to you in the first place?
Client:	[shrugs his shoulders] Nobody else to talk to.
Therapist:	Were you the only person at the party then?
Client:	Of course not. The room was quite crowded.
Therapist:	How was she behaving towards you?
Client:	She was bright and bubbly I would say.
Therapist:	How did you respond?
Client:	I tried to be bright and bubbly back but I was thinking, 'I fancy you but I know you don't fancy me.'
Therapist:	What happened with those thoughts in mind?

Client: I struggled to continue the conversation and things started getting a little bit awkward and then she drifted off towards someone else.

Therapist: Is it possible that she might have stayed longer in your company if you had held up your end of the conversation?

Client: It's possible.

Therapist: Is it also possible that she was talking to you in the first place because she might have fancied you?

Client: Yes, that's possible too. Okay, I know what you're driving at. I'm willing to concede just a little that she may have been attracted to me and I messed things up.

When clients have little or no conviction in their new adaptive beliefs, it can be very difficult for them to extract any positive information from their daily experiences; therefore, the therapist needs to be alert in every session to help her clients identify schema-supporting information, i.e. for them to be open-minded rather than closed-minded in processing information which support their new beliefs.

89

Acting 'as if'

This refers to a client acting as if his new belief was true even though he may not strongly believe it at the present time. Acting in support of a new belief strengthens it, which encourages further schema-consistent behaviour which then, in turn, further strengthens the belief – and so on until it is internalized. The client is advised to pick a particular situation or arena in which to start acting 'as if' rather than attempt to promote his 'new self' straight away in many situations as he is highly likely to feel overwhelmed with the immensity of the task he has taken on. McKay and Fanning recommend that

> for your first arena, pick an area of your life in which you feel relatively safe. Don't try to tackle your most intense relationships or the responsibilities that you find most stressful. Look for a clearly defined part of your life in which you have a pretty high degree of control, with ample opportunities to put your new beliefs and rules into action.
>
> (McKay and Fanning, 1991: 112)

For example, a client whose new core belief was 'I can be efficient and organized' chose to clean the interior of his car as a first and safe step in acting in support of his new belief and then, over the following weeks, looked for other avoided chores to tackle in and outside his house before moving on to more challenging areas of his life such as putting his finances in order. Acting 'as if' eventually becomes 'I am': 'you really do become what you pretend to be' (McKay and Fanning, 1991: 119). I (MN) sometimes act 'as if' I am more confident than I really am when addressing a large audience; this helps me to keep my nervousness under control and improve my performance so that I do actually start to feel more confident during the presentation.

A major difficulty in acting 'as if' is the unfamiliarity and strangeness of the new behaviour, which some clients say makes them feel like a 'phoney', and they conclude that 'This is not me'. This difficulty can lead to client discouragement to continue acting 'as if'. However, the therapist can reassure her clients that feeling strange or unfamiliar is a natural part of the change process and encourage them to continue by learning to tolerate these uncomfortable feelings during this transitional phase from old to new ways of behaving. Acting differently indicates newness, not phoniness. Hauck (1982) suggests that what clients regard as phoney behaviour is nothing more than breaking in a new pair of shoes.

90

Historical test of the new core belief

Maladaptive core beliefs are usually formed in childhood and therefore the client may have collected a lot of evidence over the years to support them. Undertaking a retrospective survey of the client's life can help her to uncover evidence that supports her new core belief. Padesky (1994) suggests dividing the client's life into time periods (e.g. 0–2, 3–5, 6–12 years), and recommends starting the survey when the client was a baby or small child as she is unlikely to condemn herself during this period. This technique is usually employed when the client has begun to make progress in the present on strengthening her core adaptive beliefs (Beck, 1995). In the following example, the client is examining her teenage years (13–18 years):

Therapist: Can you think of any evidence that supports your new core belief 'I am a reasonably likeable person' in this period of your life?

Client: It's hard to think of any. I was generally lonely and miserable.

Therapist: Was that because you were off school for considerable periods with all the illnesses you had?

Client: That didn't help, that's for sure.

Therapist: Did anyone from school come to see you at home when you were ill?

Client: A few girls from my class came to see me.

Therapist: Was that because they liked you or were they just doing their duty for the school, so to speak?

Client: Well, if they were doing their duty for the school they would have been polite and not stayed long. No, they were friendly towards me. We chatted and laughed for a few hours. Sometimes they stayed quite late in the evening.

Therapist: So they came more than once then? [client nods] What do you think might have happened if you had

	not been off school for long periods with your ill health?
Client:	There's a good chance I would have had more friends. I never thought of that.
Therapist:	Something else to think about too: having frequent illnesses and being off school for considerable periods led to a lot of social isolation; these were facts of your teenage years. Did you turn these facts against yourself to prove you were unlikeable?
Client:	Thinking about it now, I'm sure that's what I did. Illness and isolation were not my fault. I could still be likeable even though I was not enjoying life that much at the time or had many friends.

Padesky and Greenberger state that 'it is not necessary to identify many experiences that support the new schema; even a few are meaningful to clients. Ideally, clients find one or two experiences per age period' (1995: 150).

91

Challenging each thought in the downward arrow procedure

In Point 81 we demonstrated the downward arrow procedure to uncover a core belief. While using the downward arrow we noted it was very important for the therapist to accept each thought revealed as temporarily true, otherwise challenging each one as it appears will prevent the therapist from reaching the bottom line (core belief). However, once the bottom line has been uncovered, the therapist can now help the client to challenge each thought in order to modify it (Blackburn and Davidson, 1995; Burns, 1999). To return to the example in Point 81, the client is very worried about her husband's sudden willingness to stay late at work:

Thought: He might be having an affair.

Adaptive response: He might be but, on the other hand, he might be working late for perfectly legitimate reasons. Instead of torturing myself over this issue I will ask him why he has chosen now to start working late.

Thought: Well he's going to run off with the bitch.

Adaptive response: I'm running ahead of myself. I need to establish if he is having an affair and will run off with her – two separate issues. Calling her a bitch won't make me feel better and overlooks the fact that it takes two to tango. Based on what I know of my husband in the last ten years I very much doubt he is having an affair.

Thought: I'll be all alone, unwanted.

Adaptive response: I won't be all alone or unwanted. My children and friends will be there for me if he did run off – I can depend on them in times of crisis. I'm painting too gloomy a picture. I'm quite a strong person deep down so I'll be able to soldier on if he does leave me. I won't be moping around saying 'Poor me' all over the place. So when I say I'll be unwanted, I'll still want me. I'm not going to desert me even if he has.

Core belief: That I'm unattractive, repulsive.

Adaptive response: This is really going over the top. I may not be attractive to my husband any longer but that doesn't make *me* unattractive. I had my fair share of relationships before I met my husband and I've had the come-on several times while I've been married but I was never interested as I love my husband. As for being repulsive, this is absurd. I'm not thinking straight. An accurate description of myself is that I am attractive and I will regularly remind myself of that. I can pull men if I want to and if my husband has left me, then there will be new opportunities for me.

The client established that her husband's reasons for working late were indeed work-related, not because he was having an affair with a colleague and her worries disappeared. However, she found that doing this exercise provided her with a coping strategy if her husband did leave at some future date and helped to strengthen her adaptive belief about herself.

92

Rational–emotional role play

Clients often complain of a tension between 'head thinking' and 'gut thinking'. The former refers to a light conviction in new adaptive core beliefs ('I know the new core belief is rational and sensible and will help me but . . .') while the latter focuses on a deep conviction in the old maladaptive core beliefs ('my old belief really feels like the truth about me'). Rational–emotional role play is a procedure which encourages the client to strengthen her conviction in her new belief and weaken her conviction in her old one. This is done by the client first attempting to convince herself that her old core belief ('I'm stupid') is true by marshalling all the evidence that appears to support it and then, second, challenging this evidence point by point in order to develop more balanced and realistic interpretations of the same evidence to buttress her new adaptive core belief ('I'm a reasonably intelligent person'). Kuehlwein states that the client should challenge the evidence 'vehemently and firmly', and 'once the therapist is satisfied that the client has explored this second side fully, he checks for a reduction in belief level in the old core belief and in the accompanying distress. If it does not occur, the exercise may be repeated' (2002: 27).

It is highly unlikely that clients will be unable to carry out this procedure without prompting from the therapist to gather *all* the evidence that supports her old belief ('Don't forget that one of the reasons you believe you're stupid is because you left school with only basic qualifications') and to ensure that her challenges to this evidence are considered and balanced ('Do you think you are defining intelligence solely on the basis of academic qualifications and overlooking the fact that intelligence involves a wide variety of factors? For example, you're skilled at DIY, car mechanics and have never been in debt. Are these things signs of intelligence?'). At times, the therapist may need to demonstrate rational–emotional role play before the client attempts it.

Another example of rational–emotional role play is devil's advocate disputing (Dryden, 1995). In this technique, the client states his new core belief ('I'm generally a successful person') and his present level of conviction in it ('60 per cent'). The therapist attempts, with increasing forcefulness, to undermine the client's conviction in his new belief ('You've had more setbacks than successes recently, so how in heaven's name can you call yourself successful?'). The client is encouraged to counter each of the therapist's arguments vigorously with a strong defence of his new belief ('My definition of a successful person includes setbacks. Learning from each setback is a sign of success') until the therapist has no arguments to present. If the client finds it difficult to deal with a particular argument of the therapist's, she will stop the exercise temporarily in order to help the client find a strong counter-argument and then resume the exercise. At the end of the exercise, the client re-rates his level of conviction in his new core belief. If it has gone up considerably or a little, stayed the same or even decreased, the reasons for each outcome need to elicited and discussed.

Learning self-acceptance

Clients often describe themselves in global terms (e.g. 'I'm not good enough'): 'an image of the self *as a whole person*, rather than a differentiated flexible appreciation of varying qualities or aspects of the self. By definition, it is negative or derogatory; the person is weighed in the balance and found wanting' (Fennell, 1997: 2; emphasis in original). Global ratings of the self can never capture its complexity or totality (this applies equally to positive core beliefs: calling oneself 'a genius' may be correct in your particular field, like mathematics or physics, but it does not accurately describe every aspect of your life or personality). A trait, attribute, behaviour or performance does not equal the person; when clients conclude that it does they are making the 'part equals whole' error such as 'My performance in that situation was inferior, so that makes *me* inferior'.

Self-acceptance means rating aspects of the self, but not the self on the basis of these aspects: 'My performance in that situation was inferior judged by the feedback and evaluation forms which I want to learn from in order to improve my performance, but my performance can never sum me up as a person.' It also means looking at oneself in the round by acknowledging one's positive qualities *and* shortcomings and attempting to change the latter if so desired, and frequently reminding oneself that human fallibility cannot be eradicated (so do not waste time trying!) but that the incidence of fallible behaviour can be reduced by learning from one's mistakes in order to make fewer of them (self-condemnation for making mistakes will add nothing of value to this learning process). In the following dialogue, the therapist helps the client to strengthen his existing positive core belief by adding self-acceptance to it:

Therapist: You generally see yourself as what you call a 'can-do guy'.

Client: Yes, I get things done. When I put my mind to it I usually see it through but then I come up against something I can't seem to deal with and . . . I don't know, I just seem to get all despairing and end up seeing myself as a failure.

Therapist: How would you like to cope when you come up against something you can't seem to deal with?

Client: Well, accept that this is one nut I can't crack no matter how hard I try and not get all upset about it.

Therapist: Would you also like to accept yourself for not being able to crack this particular nut or any other un-crackable nuts that may lie in the future?

Client: That seems much more preferable than calling myself a failure and all that goes with it.

Therapist: Okay, what would you need to add to your belief 'I'm a can-do guy' in order to remind yourself of that?

Client: Hmm . . . Something like 'I'm a can-do guy but not always'. That seems all right, that might work.

Therapist: How might you strengthen that belief in your mind?

Client: Keep on going over it so when I do come up against the next difficulty it will be my safety net, so to speak.

The client kept a 'can-do but not always' diary to note his accomplishments and record his difficulties without despair or self-denigration. At the follow-up appointments (see Point 99), the client said that the addition of the 'but not always' to his existing belief had 'helped me see the value of self-acceptance and I spend much less time now dwelling on my failures or setbacks'.

Unlike self-esteem, self-acceptance does not involve a loss of identity (Neenan and Dryden, 2002a). 'Esteem' is derived from the verb 'to estimate', which means to give something or someone a rating. The concept of self-esteem suggests that a person can be rated globally (e.g. 'I'm a success because I've just been promoted and I have the respect and admiration of my colleagues'). Loss of self-esteem can lead to loss of identity if favourable conditions are reversed (the client loses her job in a company merger and has little, if any, contact with her former colleagues: 'I stare in the mirror every morning and wonder, "Who am I? Where's my life gone?"'). Self-acceptance is not based on certain criteria being met (e.g. having friends, good looks, being slim, having approval from others) in order to validate one's self-worth or identity. If self-acceptance does have an identity, it is the acknowledgement of oneself as a fallible, complex, unrateable human being – this view of oneself can remain constant whatever the circumstances in one's life. We believe that self-acceptance is one of the most important concepts that therapists can teach their clients to help them avoid rating the self by implied self-esteem.

Resistance

Client resistance

Leahy defines client resistance as 'anything in the patient's behavior, thinking, affective response, and interpersonal style that interferes with the ability of that patient to utilize the treatment and to acquire the ability to handle problems outside of therapy and after therapy has been terminated' (2001: 11). These 'interferences' may include homework non-compliance, endless 'yes, buts . . .', not adhering to the agreed session agenda, always being late for therapy or missing appointments frequently, not taking responsibility for change, focusing on issues that are not clinically relevant, being overly compliant with everything the therapist suggests, and jumping from problem to problem before any productive changes have occurred in the previous problem – these and other difficulties will militate against the client becoming his own therapist which is the ultimate goal of cognitive therapy. Kwee and Lazarus state that 'resistance is bound to occur whenever one tries to exert influence on somebody else. Otherwise therapy would be a simple job, for it would then be sufficient merely to tell the client what to do' (1986: 333).

Cognitive therapists usually tackle client resistance by taking a problem-solving approach to it, as they would do for any other problem in therapy (Golden and Dryden, 1986). Such an approach helps to maintain a collaborative relationship and avoids turning it into an adversarial one (which would probably happen if the therapist viewed resistance as a 'battle' to be fought and won). For example, a client I (MN) saw frequently replied to my questions and suggestions with 'yes, but . . .'. We contrasted the aim of the 'yes' (to change the status quo in the client's life) with the aim of the 'but' (to maintain it). The client agreed for the rest of the session to focus on only the implications of the 'yes' for herself and her life without letting the 'but' intrude. The new possibilities that emerged helped the client to strengthen her commitment to change and greatly reduced the frequency of her 'yes, but . . .' responses. In this example, I was working with the client's resistance in order to overcome it rather than fighting against it by trying to challenge her every 'yes, but . . .' with a 'smart-arse' rebuttal which might have encouraged her to dig her heels in further.

Dowd (1996) has suggested some reasons for client resistance, and we suggest some ways to tackle each resistance:

1 *When a client's personal agenda is attacked.* For example, the client's overt goal (to get back to work) may conflict with his covert and real goal (to stay off work as long as possible as he hates his job). The therapist will be focused on the overt goal while the client will be following the covert one; an understandable tension will develop in therapy. The therapist needs to be alert to 'something not quite right' between the client's expressed desire to get back to work and his continual 'let's not rush' approach. This discrepancy will need to be made explicit so therapy focuses on one agreed goal such as looking for another job or, if the client wants to keep the present one, what new attitude will he need to develop to make going to work bearable, not hateful.

2 *When the client's belief system is being forced to change too quickly.* From this perspective, it can be argued 'that resistance in therapy is expected, since it is thought to reflect natural and healthy self-protective processes that guard against changing too much, too quickly' (Vallis, 1991: 51–52; Mahoney, 1988). The client may feel that her cherished beliefs are being eroded and her sense of identity is being lost through rapid change. The pace and degree of change needs to be negotiated with the client, not set by the therapist (see therapist resistance in the next point).

3 *When the change required is part of the client's self-image.* The client might see his anger as 'making me powerful and gets me what I want' and that it intimidates others, which he enjoys. To give up his anger 'would turn me into a wimp and everyone would walk all over me'. Gaining information from the client's family and relatives of the adverse effects on them of his angry outbursts, listing the effects of prolonged anger on his physical and psychological health and discussing alternative conceptions of powerful but non-intimidatory images of masculinity may help the client to modify his current self-image ('I [therapist] could argue that a real man only becomes angry when his vital interests are at stake. You get angry over the slightest thing as if the anger controls you. How powerful a self-image is that?').

4 *When clients are highly reactant*. Reactance 'refers to a motivational force to restore lost or threatened freedoms' (Dowd, 1996: 4). Such clients are likely to react aggressively if they believe the therapist is trying to control them, telling them what to think or undermining their autonomy such as the therapist setting the homework assignments for them. With these clients, the therapist should help them to preserve their sense of autonomy and continually emphasize their freedom to choose whether or not to change particular thoughts and behaviours with such questions as 'What do *you* think *you* should do in that situation to help *you* achieve better results for *yourself*?'

Leahy suggests that if the therapist can adopt an attitude of curiosity towards clients' resistance and see it as part of the 'collaborative experience of therapy' instead of personalizing it ('Why is this client behaving like this towards me when I'm trying to help him') then 'by getting into their shoes, we can help them find the pathway out' (2001: 287).

Therapist resistance

Therapist resistance can be seen as counterproductive beliefs, emotions and behaviours that impede or undermine clients' progress. When therapists label clients as 'resistant' they may be putting the label on the wrong person. Lazarus and Fay (1982) state that resistance is the therapist's rationalization to explain his treatment failures. Some examples of therapist resistance include setting the agenda and homework unilaterally rather than through agreement; seeking to confirm his hypotheses about the client's problems instead of open-mindedly seeking to confirm, modify or reject them in the light of incoming information; rigidly, instead of creatively and flexibly, applying treatment protocols ('We should be further along than we are by session three. The client is not working hard enough. We're falling behind'); undertaking a treatment programme without adequate training or skills in a particular clinical area ('I haven't dealt with any PTSD [post traumatic stress disorder] so I'd better have a go at it'); blaming the client for every difficulty in therapy; talking or lecturing too much instead of asking questions to reveal and explore the client's viewpoint; pushing clients to set ambitious goals which will reflect the therapist's competence if they are achieved instead of settling for the more modest goals that they may want to achieve; treating clients as if their main purpose in therapy is to be an admiring audience of the therapist's 'wisdom' rather than him helping them to attain their own; and agreeing on vague goals ('I want my life to be more meaningful'), instead of clear, specific and measurable ones ('Finding a partner will give more meaning to my life'), which will probably lead to therapy meandering.

Tackling such issues can start with the therapist ensuring that he has regular supervision with a competent supervisor (audiotapes or videotapes of sessions will help to reveal these problems), having consultations with peers or more experienced colleagues, and reading to increase his understanding of resistance – both his own and his clients' (Leahy, 2001; Ellis, 2002). Harder to develop is self-awareness that alerts the therapist to his own counter-therapeutic behaviour in therapy. We would suggest that the therapist monitors his own thoughts, feelings and behaviours through the use of a Daily Thought Record (DTR) in order to detect his own resistance. Some of the following signs may indicate therapist resistance:

- Making blaming, judgemental or condemning remarks about clients may indicate that the therapist is intolerant of his clients' weaknesses and failings or that he is feeling irritable about the client's 'poor performance' because it might expose him as incompetent.
- Using scare tactics ('Look, if you're not committed to change then we'd better terminate therapy now') to coerce clients to make progress in order to prove how 'great' the therapist is or to force the pace of change as the therapist becomes easily bored with what he perceives as slow progress.
- Being unrealistic about what can be achieved in therapy ('I'm sure we can get your wife to forgive you and then get her to come back home') in order to bolster the therapist's shaky self-esteem by showing himself what 'great things' he can do for his client or because he has an underlying need for the client's approval.
- Getting involved in argumentative power struggles which can indicate that the therapist needs to be right on every issue or that 'giving in' will prove that he is weak; perceived client resistance is to be defeated, not worked with.
- Dreading or being apprehensive about the approaching appointment time ('All he ever does is moan and complain. Therapy is such a bore') or feeling relieved when the client cancels or fails to attend an appointment ('Seven days of bliss before he comes back').
- Feeling frustrated that the client wants to keep talking about his problems instead of focusing on solutions to them or cannot seem to formulate any adaptive responses to his dysfunctional thoughts and beliefs.
- Having double standards: clients who are 'fun' or easy to work are treated differently ('Don't worry about not doing the homework every week. Learning is what is important, not success or failure') from clients who are viewed as refractory and/or unlikeable ('Look! If you're not prepared to do the homework, then what's the point of you staying in therapy?')

Some therapists may be reluctant to admit that they engage in counterproductive behaviour as this will call into question their own competence, but we would suggest that such therapists accept both themselves and their clients for acting resistively. On this basis, a collaborative and productive relationship can be forged to help clients realize their goals for change. If a few therapists find that dealing with their own disturbances is inordinately difficult, then a period of personal therapy is indicated. Understanding and working through their own struggles will help therapists to better appreciate the struggles of their clients as they strive for self-change (Ellis, 2002).

In this and the previous point we have focused on client and therapist resistance as separate entities. Of course, client–therapist factors can combine to impede therapeutic progress such as when the therapist and client get on 'too well' and thereby get distracted by the more mundane tasks of therapy (Dryden *et al.*, 1999). In such cases, the paradox is that if the client improves, the 'life' of the satisfactory relationship is threatened. As a result, collusion may occur between the therapist and client to avoid making therapy as effective an endeavour as it might otherwise be. This problem can be largely overcome if the therapist first helps herself and then her client to overcome the philosophy of low frustration tolerance (i.e. learning to tolerate focusing on less enjoyable but more clinically relevant issues) implicit in this collusive short-term pleasure seeking.

Towards termination
and beyond

Relapse prevention

Instilling hope in clients that they can change is an important part of therapy, addressing the likelihood of relapse is perhaps equally as important (Dryden and Feltham, 1992). Relapse prevention originated in the treatment of substance abuse (Marlatt and Gordon, 1985) but is now applied to therapy generally. A relapse is a complete return to a previous problem state, while a lapse is a partial return to a previous problem state. By the time therapy is drawing to a close, clients will have learnt, if they did not know it already, that change is not a smooth, linear process but a series of advances and setbacks. Therefore, relapse prevention – we prefer the term 'relapse reduction' as it more accurately describes the post-therapy progress of fallible human beings – is a realistic strategy to pursue by pinpointing future situations (e.g. interpersonal strife, intense negative feelings, being alone) that could trigger a relapse and helping clients to develop coping plans in order to deal with these situations (these coping plans are essentially the tools and techniques they have already learnt in therapy).

Clients can imagine themselves in these situations and rehearse their coping strategies (these exercises can be carried out as if they were happening in the present rather than the future). For example, a client who said that he would be tempted to start drinking again after a row with his partner because he would have difficulty tolerating his angry feelings, wrote his alternative thoughts and behaviours on a card: 'Call a friend from AA [Alcoholics Anonymous] to talk things through'; 'Go to a quiet part of the house to calm down'; 'Listen to relaxing music'; 'Go to the gym'; 'Forcefully remind myself that I don't need alcohol to help me through a bad situation. I am determined to face it with a clear head'; 'When I've calmed down, talk to my partner without name-calling, self-condemnation or shouting and apologize for any unpleasant behaviour I may have engaged in.'

Clients can learn that a lapse (e.g. having a drink, not keeping to a diet) does not automatically lead to a relapse if they are prepared to deal with it as soon as it has occurred by accepting that lapses are part of progress, by drawing out the lessons that can be learned from the slip to improve coping strategies in vulnerable situations (e.g. changes undertaken are not yet complete, relapse is a product of choice even if the choice is not always apparent or conscious [Ellis *et al.*, 1988]), and by avoiding all-or-nothing thinking ('Once a drunk, always a drunk'; 'As I've wrecked my diet, there's no point keeping to it') as such thinking usually turns a lapse into a relapse (Beck *et al.*, 1993). Lapses/relapses are incidents in the change process, not its whole story which some discouraged clients can come to believe. Relapse prevention helps clients to understand that slips are opportunities for learning rather than signs of personal failure and therefore after a slip they can put themselves 'back on track' (Marlatt and Gordon, 1985). Padesky and Greenberger (1995) state that outcomes in therapy are not only measured by treatment success but also by relapse prevention.

97

Termination

The end of therapy is often discussed at its outset: by working with the therapist, the client will learn a range of self-help skills to implement both in and between sessions in order to become his own problem-solver and will terminate therapy in that capacity. As the client gains both confidence and competence in managing his difficulties, sessions are tapered off (e.g. from weekly to fortnightly to monthly) with the therapist now reconceptualizing her role as the client's coach or consultant (the client has largely taken over her original role). It can be useful to have a 'countdown' approach to termination by reminding the client (and the therapist) in each session of how many sessions are left of the agreed treatment programme in order to gain maximum therapeutic benefit from them. A rush to termination or an arbitrary decision on the therapist's part ('We'll make this session the last one') can undo the benefits of therapy:

> For this reason, it is important that the process of completion of therapy be handled as effectively and as smoothly as possible. When the conclusion of therapy is handled well, the patient is more likely to consolidate gains and to generalize strategies for handling future problems.
>
> (Beck *et al.*, 1979: 317)

The client can be asked to summarize his gains from therapy, in particular those ideas and techniques he found especially valuable; these gains can be written down on a card and kept in the client's purse or wallet for easy access. For example, the client says that 'putting my thinking under the spotlight really showed me how much of an all-or-nothing thinker I really was'. Two ideas he will particularly hold on to are that (1) thoughts are hypotheses, not facts, and 'therefore I can change them by examining them', and that (2) he can choose how he reacts to situations: 'Before cognitive therapy, I believed that situations made me angry, but now I realize I have more options to choose from in deciding how I want to react.' A technique he found very helpful was progressive muscle relaxation (systematically tensing and relaxing the major muscle groups of the body while maintaining a slow breathing rate) 'as I can't be angry and relaxed at the same time and I'd rather be relaxed'. An action plan was developed to deal with future problematic situations which might trigger prolonged angry outbursts (see previous point on relapse prevention).

Clients often have concerns about termination which the therapist needs to address. Some of these concerns are:

- *'I won't be able to cope on my own.'* The client has already been coping on her own by carrying out homework assignments; also, she will still be able to hear the voice of the therapist providing encouragement and support, so she will not be psychologically on her own and therefore can engage in an imaginal consultation with the therapist when struggling to cope in times of difficulty. The client can view her prediction as in need of empirical testing (like all her other predictions in therapy) by striking out alone.
- *'Not all my problems have been sorted out.'* Therapy is not intended to sort out all the client's problems, just some of them. The client's self-help skills can be applied to these other problems post-therapy; to have resolved all the client's problems before he leaves therapy undermines the idea of becoming a self-therapist and risks the client becoming dependent upon the therapist to do his problem-solving for him.
- *'I'm not cured yet.'* Again, therapy is never intended to 'cure' the client but to reduce the frequency, intensity and duration of his problems; in other words, to manage them more effectively (Beck *et al.*, 1979). Self-management becomes more effective through the client applying his cognitive and behavioural skills in problematic situations and learning from his experiences.
- *'I haven't told you what the real problem is.'* This statement can give the impression that therapy was a prelude to the 'real stuff' (e.g. sexual abuse) being explored, but now it is too late as therapy has come to an end. The therapist can explore briefly why the client has revealed this issue at the last minute and whether or not to extend counselling; decide to keep to the agreed problem list, not add to it; and suggest that the client can contact him at a later date for another course of counselling focusing on the 'real stuff',

or refer the client to another therapist. The therapist should not feel trapped or blackmailed into automatically extending therapy.

- *'I'm getting all anxious again, so it can't be time for me to go.'* As termination nears, some clients feel understandably apprehensive about going it alone and see themselves 'falling apart' post-therapy. These fears trigger a reactivation of their presenting symptoms which gives the impression to these clients that they are actually getting worse, not better. They can be reminded that feelings are not facts ('Just because I fear relapsing as soon as therapy ends does not mean that I will'), that this is a common experience as termination approaches, that they have made considerable progress as self-therapists despite their present apprehension, and that what happens after therapy is not yet 'written' – their self-therapy diaries can tell of coping rather than of catastrophe.

While clients are usually appreciative of the therapist's efforts ('I couldn't have done it without your help'), it is important for the therapist to resist the temptation of taking too much credit for the client's success ('Well, now you come to mention it . . .') and place the major credit where it belongs – with the client. Wills and Sanders (1997) suggest pointing out to clients that they have been working on their problems for twenty-four hours a day, seven days a week while the therapist has only put in session time of, for example, eight, ten or twelve hours. Finally, termination should not be viewed by the therapist as an inevitably sad or wrenching experience for clients; some clients, while pleased with their progress, will want a business-like end to therapy.

98

Maintaining gains from therapy

Achieving one's goals is not the same process as maintaining them (e.g. getting fit, then staying fit; losing weight, then keeping to the new weight). Some clients might believe that once therapy is terminated their therapeutic gains will 'magically' stay intact without any further input from them, that they deserve a prolonged rest after all their hard work in therapy, or that therapy was a discrete, crisis-driven episode that they now can thankfully put behind them (Neenan and Dryden, in press). In our experience, clients can quickly fall back into old self-defeating patterns of thinking and behaving by taking their 'eye off the ball', i.e. not practising their hard-won cognitive therapy skills, so a maintenance outlook needs to be developed by them to forestall such an outcome.

To initiate a discussion on this issue, the therapist can ask: 'How will you keep your progress going after therapy ends?' or 'Does ten sessions of therapy provide you with a lifelong guarantee that you will never slip back?' In essence, a maintenance outlook, idiosyncratically tailored, is that in order to keep and strengthen one's gains from therapy continuing effort is required from the client; in other words, self-therapy as a way of life. For example, one client's maintenance message was 'use it or lose it' while another client's was 'check regularly my cognitive circuits' (he worked as an electrician). Beck (1995) suggests that clients can schedule self-therapy sessions, modelled on CT sessions, where they set an agenda which will include designing and reviewing homework tasks, assessing progress, dealing with current difficulties and troubleshooting future ones. Clients can put the dates for self-therapy sessions in their diary.

Clients can be alert for warning signs that they might be heading for a setback and have a prepared action plan to hand (family and friends can also be involved in looking out for warning signs). Some examples:

- A client feels hot and uncomfortable in a supermarket queue and has the urge to 'run outside' to escape an imagined catastrophe. However, the client vigorously reminds himself that his panicky symptoms are harmless, not dangerous, based on the experiments he conducted in therapy: 'My panicky feelings will pass quickly like they've always done and I'll be fine as always, so keep calm.' He also remembers the three-minute rule he learnt in therapy: 'Because adrenaline from your fight-or-flight reaction takes three minutes or less to be metabolized, your panic must end unless new anxious thoughts cause the release of more adrenaline' (McKay *et al.*, 1997: 95). Controlling his thoughts controlled his panic; the client stayed in the queue and his symptoms subsided.

- A wife points out to her husband that 'you're doing it again, darling', i.e. brooding on mistakes he made at work. Past mistakes resulted in low mood and self-condemnation. Now, his wife's 'nudge' encourages him to go over a valuable lesson from therapy: 'Mistakes are inevitable; getting upset over them is not.' With this thought in mind, he makes a few notes on how he can rectify and learn from his mistakes.

- A client starts to feel 'clingy' again in her relationship as old fears of being unlovable and abandoned resurface. In order to strengthen her belief that she does not need love in order to be happy or to prove her worth, she spends time alone. This reaffirms her ability to enjoy her own company. As the client tells her partner: 'When the clinginess goes, we have a much better time.'

Another way of maintaining and strengthening therapeutic gains is for the client to teach others some of the cognitive skills he learnt in therapy, e.g. explaining to a friend that she should consider *all* the factors that contributed to the end of her marriage instead of blaming herself for the break up: 'I learnt in therapy to look at the whole picture, not just my part in it' (see Point 55 on reattribution). Through teaching others, the client continues to teach himself valuable problem-solving methods. It is important that the client does not present himself to others as a 'know-all' or paragon as this is likely to alienate them rather than encourage them to listen and learn. Clients can also use their CT skills in other problem areas of their life they may have been avoiding tackling or which have recently arisen – e.g., respectively, standing up to an overbearing work colleague or firmly requesting new neighbours to turn down their loud music.

Cognitive therapy skills are not only used for overcoming present and future problems but also in the service of ambition and realizing important life goals (Neenan and Dryden, 2002b). Psychological difficulties are dealt with first otherwise they will interfere with clients' attempts to achieve these goals. For example, a client who entered therapy to tackle a bout of depression and worry decided, on recovery, that he wanted to fulfil his long-standing desire to be self-employed. He developed an action plan to help him achieve this goal. In follow-up appointments (see next point) his recovery was monitored, as was to be expected, but the therapist also spent some time discussing the client's progress towards becoming self-employed and how he was dealing with roadblocks he encountered along the way.

99

Follow-up

How will the therapist know whether or not her clients are maintaining their therapeutic gains or determine the efficacy of her treatment approach if she never sees them again once therapy ends? Follow-up appointments such as in three, six and twelve months' time can be offered to clients in order to monitor their progress as self-therapists – how firmly have they consolidated their gains from therapy? The therapist should allow sufficient time to elapse before arranging a follow-up in order to determine the extent of the client's progress without the therapist's support (Cormier and Cormier, 1985). For example, if the client has spent ten sessions in therapy over a period of three months, then the first follow-up can be scheduled in three months' time. It should be made clear to clients that follow-up sessions are not therapy sessions. Follow-up also offers clients a longer-term perspective from which to reflect on their experience of therapy and what they have learnt from it. A client I (MN) saw at a twelve-month follow-up appointment said that it was only now that she was beginning to really appreciate and benefit from what she had learnt in therapy about replacing self-esteem with self-acceptance (see Point 93 for a discussion of these two concepts). Follow-up provides useful information for the therapist in reviewing her work with clients and finding out what they found helpful and unhelpful about it (Dryden and Feltham, 1992).

Some clients feel safer about terminating therapy as their therapeutic progress is still being 'kept an eye on' by the therapist, though follow-ups are not meant to keep therapy going under the guise of monitoring progress. Sometimes clients find that difficulties which have emerged post-therapy are, after a period of personal struggle with them, too difficult to deal with on their own; if this is the case, then they can contact the therapist to arrange an appointment ahead of the official follow-up. Such a contingency arrangement is usually agreed on in the final session of formal therapy. If the client has deteriorated since the end of therapy, the reasons for this should be elicited (e.g.

the client has experienced a number of significant setbacks in his life which he describes as 'doing my head in') and he can be offered a brief top-up or revision period of therapy – not another full course of CT as this may convey to the client that all his previously hard-won progress was actually an illusion ('I obviously did not understand *anything* about cognitive therapy the first time around').

Cognitive therapy:
is it just for clients?

100

Practising what you preach

Do cognitive therapists practise cognitive therapy on themselves when they encounter difficulties, both inside and outside therapy? Not always. Our experience of training and supervising cognitive therapists shows us that some individuals have either no idea of how to apply CT to themselves or no wish to – therapy is something that they do to 'them' (i.e. clients) and is not performed on themselves. This attitude is unfortunate as it can lead these therapists to practise CT without a genuine conviction in it, not appreciate the difficulties their clients have in implementing CT skills in their everyday lives (and likely to call them 'resistant' when progress is stalled), and do what is necessary to be a competent practitioner (further training, attending workshops, regular supervision) but lack the experiential element in their CT practice. Furthermore, when these therapists opt for personal therapy they are likely to choose a different approach such as psychodynamic therapy: 'I know all about cognitive therapy. I do it every day. I want to try something new and different for myself.' We would make three observations about this response:

1 It is a rash person who claims to 'know all about cognitive therapy' (maybe it is time for him to retire). We doubt that Aaron Beck, who developed CT, would make this claim as he is continually setting himself new challenges in cognitive therapy (Weishaar, 2002).
2 Trying 'something new and different for myself' would be receiving CT as a client instead of delivering it as a therapist. Padesky points out that a 'final process [after training and supervision] that enhances the competency of cognitive therapists is participating in cognitive therapy as a client. To fully understand the process of the therapy, there is no substitute for using cognitive therapy methods on oneself' (1996: 288). Some CT therapists see a more appealing substitute.
3 Practising CT but entering a non-CT approach for personal therapy suggests a schism between head and heart: the head responds to the

empirically validated, active-directive, time-limited, structured approach of CT for dealing with a heavy caseload but the heart yearns for untrammelled exploration and discussion, divested of forms, inventories, agendas, session targets, goals and homework 'where I can really be myself' as one therapist said to us. While the therapist may be technically proficient in her practice of CT, she is presenting an inauthentic self to her clients.

Persons (1989), in her book *Cognitive Therapy in Practice*, devotes a chapter to 'Cognitive therapy for the cognitive therapist' and stresses the need for therapists to work on their own dysfunctional thoughts and beliefs that might hamper their work with clients. Therapists can use the Daily Thought Record (DTR) forms to detect, challenge and change their dysfunctional thinking and thereby moderate their disturbed feelings. For example:

- *The anger-inducing 'My clients should work as hard as I do'.* Therapy is not based on an equivalence of effort: the amount of effort that clients put into therapy is proportionate to the gains they will make. This is their choice, not the therapist's.
- *The anxiety-provoking 'What if I can't help my clients? They'll think I'm useless'.* It is highly unlikely that the therapist will not be able to help any of her clients, and what kind of help is required is mutually decided, not therapist-driven. Frequent progress reviews will help to establish if clients believe they are getting better. The therapist will only know if her clients think she is useless by asking them, not through mind-reading. If one or two of her clients do tell her she is 'useless' because therapy did not work out for them, she can remind herself that this is a global and therefore inaccurate judgement of herself and then ask for specific feedback on the 'uselessness' of her clinical performance.
- *The guilt-creating 'I'm a bad therapist for not preventing my client from relapsing'.* The therapist believes he is omnipotent and can control the client's destiny. Relapse prevention is the therapist's responsibility to address and the client's to implement. Also, relapse prevention is not to be taken literally: some lapses/relapses are likely (see Point 96). Like the clients in the previous point, the therapist is making a global and therefore inaccurate judgement but, in this instance, it is of his role, not himself. Client setbacks are to

be expected and reviewed when they occur; calling himself a 'bad therapist' will add nothing of value to the review.

- *The locked-in-agreement of 'My client's right: you are worthless without a partner'.* A dysfunctional agreement that will keep both client and therapist stuck. The therapist needs to acknowledge that she holds such a belief and forcefully remind herself of what she has taught to other clients with low self-esteem problems: namely, that one's worth is not dependent on having a partner, lots of friends, good looks, expensive cars, designer clothes, etc. Self-worth is inherent (a person is born with it); therefore, it does not have to be earned or made conditional, so partners can come and go but one's worth is constant and non-negotiable. Once the therapist has convinced herself of this viewpoint, then she can help her client in a similar way.

By dealing with their own cognitive vulnerabilities and upsetting feelings, therapists remain congruent with what they say and do and thereby act authentically with their clients.

Initial case conceptualization of a client with discrete (situation-specific) social phobia*

Predisposing factors forming client's cognitive vulnerability to future situations where his nervousness might be evident and he wants to conceal it

Earlier experiences

Remembers fear of being in the spotlight at school as this led to physical punishment by the teachers when he got things wrong: 'I stood there crying; it was so humiliating.' Worried at college that he might make a fool of himself by appearing weak or nervous and be ostracized for it.

Tacit message: 'Don't show nervousness to others'

Core beliefs, underlying assumptions and rules

'I'm weak' (core belief)

'If I keep myself under control, then I'll be seen as competent and strong' (positive assumption)

'If I show weakness or nervousness, then I'll be ridiculed and rejected' (negative assumption)

'I must come across to others as a competent person' (rule)

Strategies to avoid activating core belief
Project image of strength and resilience
Work hard to get ahead in life
Remove imperfections in himself

Precipitating event
Being appointed as chairman of an important committee and feeling very apprehensive about it

Core belief and negative assumption activated
He will be exposed as weak leading to ridicule and rejection

Situation
Waiting to sign the minutes of the last meeting (being in the spotlight)

| Factors maintaining client's problem | Negative automatic thoughts (NATS)
'My hand will shake uncontrollably'
'I'll be seen as nervous and out of control'
'My credibility will be destroyed'
'They won't want me as chairman' | | |

↗	↕	↕	↖
Self-consciousness/ mind-reading	*Safety behaviours*	*Physical symptoms*	*Emotions*
'They can see how nervous I feel'	Keep tight control of himself Have pen ready Rush signature	Heart racing Mind spinning Tightness in chest Dry mouth Trembling	Near panic

Note: * 'The essential feature of Social Phobia is a marked and persistent fear of social or performance situations in which embarrassment may occur. Exposure to the social or performance situation almost invariably provokes an immediate anxiety response' (American Psychiatric Association, 1994: 411).

Daily Thought Record (DTR) of client with discrete social phobia

Situation	Negative automatic thoughts	Emotions	Alternative and balanced thoughts	How do you feel now?
Describe clearly and concisely	Rate believability of thoughts (0–100%)	Rate intensity of emotions (0–100%)	Rate believability of alternative thoughts (0–100%)	Re-rate intensity of emotions (0–100%)
Waiting for the minutes of the last meeting to be passed to me for signing	My hand will shake uncontrollably (90%)	Anxiety (90%)	It has shaken in the past but never uncontrollably (70%)	Anxiety (40%)
	I'll be seen as nervous and out of control (90%)		I'm mind-reading again. If I want to know how they really see me, then I'll ask them (70%)	
	My credibility will be destroyed (95%)		It will take something far more serious than my hand shaking for my credibility to be destroyed (75%)	
	They won't want me as chairman (90%)		They voted me chairman and, as far as I know, they still want me (75%)	

Appendix 3

Homework assignment form for client with discrete social phobia

1 What is the assignment? (State when, where and how often the assignment is to be carried out)

This Friday evening at the meeting I will wait for the minutes to be passed to me by the secretary, pick up my pen and slowly write my signature in order to linger in the spotlight.

2 What is the purpose of the assignment? (This should follow on from the work done in the session and be linked to the client's goal)

To test my catastrophic prediction that my hand will shake uncontrollably if I do the above things rather than engage in my usual behaviour of snatching the minutes from the secretary and having my pen ready to write my signature as quickly as possible to get myself out of the spotlight. In other words, I'm going to drop my safety behaviours.

3 Troubleshooting obstacles to homework completion

Potential obstacle: I'll get so anxious about things going hideously wrong if I drop my safety behaviours that I'll avoid doing the assignment.

Response: I'm going to do this assignment come hell or high water! I've had enough of living with this fear.

4 Contingency planning if assignment proves too difficult to complete

Do what I can. Note down my thoughts and feelings that blocked me from carrying out the assignment. Remind myself that these assignments are about me learning more about my problem and how to overcome it; they are not about success or failure in terms of the assignment or myself.

References

Alford, B. A. and Beck, A. T. (1997) *The Integrative Power of Cognitive Therapy*. New York: Guilford.

Altrows, I. F. (2002) 'Rational emotive and cognitive behavior therapy with adult male offenders', *Journal of Rational–Emotive and Cognitive-Behavior Therapy*, 20 (3/4): 201–222.

American Psychiatric Association (1994) *Diagnostic and Statistical Manual of Mental Disorders*, 4th edn. Washington, DC: American Psychiatric Association.

Barlow, D. H. and Cerny, J. A. (1988) *Psychological Treatment of Panic*. New York: Guilford.

Barlow, D. H. and Craske, M. G. (1989) *Mastery of your Anxiety and Panic*. Albany, N.Y.: Graywind Publications.

Beck, A. T. (1976) *Cognitive Therapy and the Emotional Disorders*. New York: New American Library.

Beck, A. T. (1987) 'Cognitive models of depression', *Journal of Cognitive Psychotherapy*, 1 (1): 5–37.

Beck, A. T. (1988) *Love is Never Enough*. New York: Harper & Row.

Beck, A. T., Steer, R. A. and Brown, G. K. (1996) *Beck Depression Inventory*, 2nd edn. San Antonio, TX.: The Psychological Corporation.

Beck, A. T., Emery, G. and Greenberg, R. L. (1985) *Anxiety Disorders and Phobias: A Cognitive Perspective*. New York: Basic Books.

Beck, A. T., Freeman, A. and Associates (1990) *Cognitive Therapy of Personality Disorders*. New York: Guilford.

Beck, A. T., Epstein, N., Brown, G. and Steer, R. A. (1988) 'An inventory for measuring clinical anxiety: psychometric properties', *Journal of Consulting and Clinical Psychology*, 56: 893–897.

Beck, A. T., Rush, A. J., Shaw, B. F. and Emery, G. (1979) *Cognitive Therapy of Depression*. New York: Guilford.

Beck, A. T., Wright, F. D., Newman, C. F. and Liese, B. S. (1993) *Cognitive Therapy of Substance Abuse*. New York: Guilford.

Beck, J. S. (1995) *Cognitive Therapy: Basics and Beyond*. New York: Guilford.

Blackburn, I. M. and Davidson, K. (1995) *Cognitive Therapy for Depression and Anxiety* (amended). Oxford: Blackwell Scientific Publications.

Blackburn, I. M. and Twaddle, V. (1996) *Cognitive Therapy in Action*. London: Souvenir Press.

Bruch, M. (1998) 'The development of case formulation approaches', in M. Bruch and F. W. Bond (eds), *Beyond Diagnosis: Case Formulation Approaches in CBT*. Chichester: Wiley.

Burns, D. D. (1989) *The Feeling Good Handbook*. New York: William Morrow.

Burns, D. D. (1999) *Feeling Good: The New Mood Therapy*, 2nd edn. New York: Avon Books.

Butler, G. and Hope, T. (1996) *Manage Your Mind*. Oxford: Oxford University Press.

Clark, D. A. (1995) 'Perceived limitations of standard cognitive therapy: a consideration of efforts to revise Beck's theory and therapy', *Journal of Cognitive Psychotherapy*, 9 (3): 153–172.

Clark, D. A. (1997) 'Is cognitive therapy ill-founded? A commentary on Lyddon and Weill', *Journal of Cognitive Psychotherapy*, 11 (2): 91–98.

Clark, D. A. and Steer, R. A. (1996) 'Empirical status of the cognitive model of anxiety and depression', in P. M. Salkovskis (ed.), *Frontiers of Cognitive Therapy*. New York: Guilford.

Clark, D. M. (1989) 'Anxiety states: panic and generalized anxiety', in K. Hawton, P. M. Salkovskis, J. Kirk and D. M. Clark (eds), *Cognitive Behaviour Therapy for Psychiatric Problems: A Practical Guide*. Oxford: Oxford University Press.

Clark, D. M. (1996) 'Panic disorder: from theory to therapy', in P. M. Salkovskis (ed.), *Frontiers of Cognitive Therapy*. New York: Guilford.

Clark, D. M. and Wells, A. (1995) 'A cognitive model of social phobia', in R. G. Heimberg, M. R. Liebowitz, D. A. Hope and F. R. Schneier (eds), *Social Phobia: Diagnosis, Assessment and Treatment*. New York: Guilford.

Cooper, M., Todd, G. and Wells, A. (2000) *Bulimia Nervosa: A Cognitive Therapy Programme for Clients*. London: Jessica Kingsley Publishers.

Cormier, W. H. and Cormier, L. S. (1985) *Interviewing Strategies for Helpers: Fundamental Skills and Cognitive Behavioral Interventions*, 2nd edn. Monterey, CA.: Brooks/Cole.

Dattilio, F. M. and Freeman, A. (1992) 'Introduction to cognitive therapy', in A. Freeman and F. M. Dattilio (eds), *Comprehensive Casebook of Cognitive Therapy*. New York: Plenum.

Dattilio, F. M. and Padesky, C. A. (1990) *Cognitive Therapy with Couples*. Sarasota, FL.: Professional Resource Exchange.

Davidson, K. (2000) *Cognitive Therapy for Personality Disorders*. Oxford: Butterworth-Heinemann.

DiGiuseppe, R. (1991a) 'Comprehensive cognitive disputing in RET', in M. E. Bernard (ed.), *Using Rational–Emotive Therapy Effectively: A Practitioner's Guide*. New York: Plenum.

DiGiuseppe, R. (1991b) 'A rational–emotive model of assessment', in M. E. Bernard (ed.), *Using Rational–Emotive Therapy Effectively: A Practitioner's Guide*. New York: Plenum.

DiGiuseppe, R. and Linscott, J. (1993) 'Philosophical differences among cognitive behavioral therapists: rationalism, constructivism, or both?', *Journal of Cognitive Psychotherapy*, 7 (2): 117–130.

Dowd, E. T. (1996) 'Resistance and reactance in cognitive therapy', *International Cognitive Therapy Newsletter*, 10 (3): 3–5.

Dryden, W. (1995) *Brief Rational Emotive Behaviour Therapy*. Chichester: Wiley.

Dryden, W. and Feltham, C. (1992) *Brief Counselling: A Practical Guide for Beginning Practitioners*. Buckingham: Open University Press.

Dryden, W., Neenan, M. and Yankura, J. (1999) *Counselling Individuals: A Rational Emotive Behavioural Handbook*, 3rd edn. London: Whurr.

Ehlers, A. and Clark, D. M. (2000) 'A cognitive model of post-traumatic stress disorder', *Behaviour Research and Therapy*, 38: 319–345.

Ellis, A. (2002) *Overcoming Resistance: A Rational Emotive Behavior Therapy Integrated Approach*, 2nd edn. New York: Springer.

Ellis, A., McInerney, J. F., DiGiuseppe, R. and Yeager, R. J. (1988) *Rational–Emotive Therapy with Alcoholics and Substance Abusers*. New York: Pergamon.

Fennell, M. J. V. (1989) 'Depression', in K. Hawton, P. M. Salkovskis, J. Kirk and D. M. Clark (eds), *Cognitive Behaviour Therapy for Psychiatric Problems: A Practical Guide*. Oxford: Oxford University Press.

Fennell, M. J. V. (1997) 'Low self-esteem: a cognitive perspective', *Behavioural and Cognitive Psychotherapy*, 25 (1): 1–25.

Fennell, M. (1999) *Overcoming Low Self-Esteem*. London: Robinson.

Flew, A. (1975) *Thinking About Thinking*. London: Fontana.

Frankl, V. E. (1985) *Man's Search for Meaning* (revised and updated). New York: Washington Square Press.

Free, M. L. (1999) *Cognitive Therapy in Groups*. Chichester: Wiley.

Freeman, A. and Dattilio, F. M. (1992) 'Cognitive therapy in the year 2000', in A. Freeman and F. M. Dattilio (eds), *Comprehensive Casebook of Cognitive Therapy*. New York: Plenum.

Freeman, A., Schrodt, G. R., Jr., Gilson, M. and Ludgate, J. W. (1993) 'Group cognitive therapy with inpatients', in J. H. Wright, M. E. Thase, A. T. Beck and J. W. Ludgate (eds), *Cognitive Therapy with Inpatients*. New York: Guilford.

Friedberg, R. D. and McClure, J. M. (2002) *Clinical Practice of Cognitive Therapy with Children and Adolescents: The Nuts and Bolts*. New York: Guilford.

Gilbert, P. (2000) *Counselling for Depression*, 2nd edn. London: Sage Publications.

Golden, W. L. and Dryden, W. (1986) 'Cognitive-behavioural therapies: commonalities, divergences and future developments', in W. Dryden and W. Golden (eds), *Cognitive-Behavioural Approaches to Psychotherapy*. London: Harper & Row.

Greenberger, D. and Padesky, C.A. (1995) *Mind Over Mood*. New York: Guilford.

Grieger, R. and Boyd, J. (1980) *Rational–Emotive Therapy: A Skills-Based Approach*. New York: Van Nostrand Reinhold.

Hauck, P. (1982) *How To Do What You Want To Do*. London: Sheldon Press.

James, I. A. (2001) 'Schema therapy: the next generation, but should it carry a health warning?', *Behavioural and Cognitive Psychotherapy*, 29 (4): 401–407.

Kennerley, H. (1997) *Overcoming Anxiety*. London: Robinson.

Kirk, J. (1989) 'Cognitive-behavioural assessment', in K. Hawton, P. M. Salkovskis, J. Kirk and D. M. Clark (eds), *Cognitive Behaviour Therapy for Psychiatric Problems: A Practical Guide*. Oxford: Oxford University Press.

Kroese, B. S., Dagnan, D. and Loumidis, K. (1997) *Cognitive-Behaviour Therapy for People with Learning Disabilities*. London: Brunner-Routledge.

Kuehlwein, K. T. (2002) 'The cognitive treatment of depression', in G. Simos (ed.), *Cognitive Behaviour Therapy: A Guide for the Practising Clinician*. Hove: Brunner-Routledge.

Kwee, M. G. T. and Lazarus, A. A. (1986) 'Multimodal therapy: the cognitive-behavioural tradition and beyond', in W. Dryden and W. Golden (eds), *Cognitive-Behavioural Approaches to Psychotherapy*. London: Harper & Row.

Laidlaw, K., Thompson, L. W., Dick-Siskin, L. and Gallagher-Thompson, D. (2003) *Cognitive Behaviour Therapy with Older People*. Chichester: Wiley.

Lazarus, A. (1984) *In the Mind's Eye*. New York: Guilford.

Lazarus, A. and Fay, A. (1982) 'Resistance or rationalization? A cognitive-behavioral perspective', in P. Wachtel (ed.), *Resistance: Psychodynamic and Behavioral Approaches*. New York: Plenum.

Leahy, R. L. (2001) *Overcoming Resistance in Cognitive Therapy*. New York: Guilford.

Leahy, R. L. and Holland, S. J. (2000) *Treatment Plans and Interventions for Depression and Anxiety Disorders*. New York: Guilford.

Lyddon, W. J. and Jones, J. V., Jr (eds) (2001) *Empirically Supported Cognitive Therapies: Current and Future Applications*. New York: Springer.

McKay, M. and Fanning, P. (1991) *Prisoners of Belief*. Oakland, CA.: New Harbinger Publications.

McKay, M., Davis, M. and Fanning, P. (1997) *Thoughts and Feelings: Taking Control of Your Moods and Your Life*, 2nd edn. Oakland, CA.: New Harbinger Publications.

Mahoney, M. J. (1988) 'The cognitive sciences and psychotherapy: patterns in a developing relationship', in K. S. Dobson (ed.), *Handbook of Cognitive-Behavioral Therapies*. New York: Guilford.

Mahoney, M. J. and Gabriel, T. J. (1987) 'Psychotherapy and the cognitive sciences: an evolving alliance', *Journal of Cognitive Psychotherapy*, 1 (1): 39–59.

Marlatt, G. A. and Gordon, J. R. (eds) (1985) *Relapse Prevention: Maintenance Strategies in the Treatment of Addictive Behaviours*. New York: Guilford.

Mooney, K. A. and Padesky, C. A. (2000) 'Applying client creativity to recurrent problems: constructing possibilities and tolerating doubt', *Journal of Cognitive Psychotherapy*, 14 (2): 149–161.

Moorey, S. (1990) 'Cognitive therapy', in W. Dryden (ed.), *Individual Therapy: A Handbook*. Milton Keynes: Open University Press.

Moorey, S. (1996) 'When bad things happen to rational people: cognitive therapy in adverse life circumstances', in P. M. Salkovskis (ed.), *Frontiers of Cognitive Therapy*. New York: Guilford.

Morrison, A. (ed.) (2001) *A Casebook of Cognitive Therapy for Psychosis*. Hove: Brunner-Routledge.

Naugle, A. E. and Follette, W. C. (1998) 'A functional analysis of trauma symptoms', in V. M. Follette, J. I. Ruzek and F. R. Abueg (eds), *Cognitive-Behavioral Therapies for Trauma*. New York: Guilford.

Neenan, M. and Dryden, W. (2000) *Essential Cognitive Therapy*. London: Whurr.

Neenan, M. and Dryden, W. (2002a) *Cognitive Behaviour Therapy: An A–Z of Persuasive Arguments*. London: Whurr.

Neenan, M. and Dryden, W. (2002b) *Life Coaching: A Cognitive Behavioural Approach*. London: Brunner-Routledge.

Neenan, M. and Dryden, W. (in press) *Cognitive Therapy in a Nutshell*. London: Sage.

Neenan, M. and Palmer, S. (1998) 'A cognitive-behavioural approach to tackling stress', *Counselling, the Journal of the British Association for Counselling*, 9 (4): 315–319.

Newman, C. F. (1989) 'Where's the evidence? A clinical tip', *International Cognitive Therapy Newsletter*, 5 (1): 4, 8.

Newman, C. F. (2000) 'Hypotheticals in cognitive psychotherapy: creative questions, novel answers, and therapeutic change', *Journal of Cognitive Psychotherapy*, 14 (2): 135–147.

Newman, C. F., Leahy, R. L., Beck, A. T., Reilly-Harrington, N. A. and Gyulai, L. (2002) *Bipolar Disorder: A Cognitive Therapy Approach*. Washington, DC: American Psychological Association.

Padesky, C. A. (1993a) 'Staff and patient education', in J. H. Wright, M. E. Thase, A. T. Beck and J. W. Ludgate (eds), *Cognitive Therapy with Inpatients*. New York: Guilford.

Padesky, C. A. (1993b) 'Socratic questioning: changing minds or guiding discovery?' A keynote address delivered at the European Congress of Behavioural and Cognitive Therapies, London, 24 September.

Padesky, C. A. (1994) 'Schema change processes in cognitive therapy', *Clinical Psychology and Psychotherapy*, 1 (5): 267–278.

Padesky, C. A. (1996) 'Developing cognitive therapist competency: teaching and supervision models', in P. M. Salkovskis (ed.), *Frontiers of Cognitive Therapy*. New York: Guilford.

Padesky, C. A. and Greenberger, D. (1995) *Clinician's Guide to Mind Over Mood*. New York: Guilford.

Persaud, R. (2003) Interview with Aaron Beck. *All in the Mind*, Radio 4, 26 March.

Persons, J. B. (1989) *Cognitive Therapy in Practice: A Case Formulation Approach*. New York: Norton.

Persons, J. B., Burns, D. D. and Perloff, J. M. (1988) 'Predictors of dropout and outcome in cognitive therapy for depression in a private practice setting', *Cognitive Therapy and Research*, 12 (6): 557–575.

Persons, J. B., Davidson, J. and Tompkins, M. A. (2001) *Essential Components of Cognitive-Behavior Therapy for Depression*. Washington, D.C.: American Psychological Association.

Safran, J. D. and Muran, J. C. (2000) *Negotiating the Therapeutic Alliance*. New York: Guilford.

Safran, J. D. and Segal, Z. V. (1990) *Interpersonal Process in Cognitive Therapy*. New York: Basic Books.

Salkovskis, P. M. (1991) 'The importance of behaviour in the maintenance of anxiety and panic: a cognitive account', *Behavioural Psychotherapy*, 19: 6–19.

Salkovskis, P. M. (1996) 'Preface', in P. M. Salkovskis (ed.), *Frontiers of Cognitive Therapy*. New York: Guilford.

Salkovskis, P. M. (1999) 'Understanding and treating obsessive-compulsive disorder', *Behaviour Research and Therapy*, 37: 529–552.

Salkovskis, P. M. and Bass, C. (1997) 'Hypochondriasis', in D. M. Clark and C. G. Fairburn (eds), *Science and Practice of Cognitive Behaviour Therapy*. Oxford: Oxford University Press.

Salkovskis, P. M. and Clark, D. M. (1991) 'Cognitive therapy for panic disorder', *Journal of Cognitive Psychotherapy*, 5 (3): 215–226.

Sperry, L. (1999) *Cognitive Behavior Therapy of DSM-IV Personality Disorders*. Philadelphia, PA.: Brunner/Mazel.

Stallard, P. (2002) *Think Good–Feel Good: A Cognitive Behaviour Therapy Workbook for Children and Young People*. Chichester: Wiley.

Tinch, C. S. and Friedberg, R. D. (1996) 'The schema identification worksheet: a guide for clients and clinicians', *International Cognitive Therapy Newsletter*, 10 (4): 1–4.

Vallis, T. M. (1991) 'Theoretical and conceptual bases of cognitive therapy', in T. M. Vallis, J. L. Howes and P. C. Miller (eds), *The Challenge of Cognitive Therapy*. New York: Plenum.

Walen, S. R., DiGiuseppe, R. and Dryden, W. (1992) *A Practitioner's Guide to Rational–Emotive Therapy*, 2nd edn. New York: Oxford University Press.

Warburton, N. (2000) *Thinking from A to Z*, 2nd edn. London: Routledge.

Weishaar, M. E. (1993) *Aaron T. Beck*. London: Sage Publications.

Weishaar, M. E. (1996) 'Developments in cognitive therapy', in W. Dryden (ed.), *Developments in Psychotherapy: Historical Perspectives*. London: Sage Publications.

Weishaar, M. E. (2002) 'The life of Aaron T. Beck, MD', in R. L. Leahy and E. T. Dowd (eds), *Clinical Advances in Cognitive Psychotherapy: Theory and Application*. New York: Springer.

Weishaar, M. E. and Beck, A. T. (1986) 'Cognitive therapy', in W. Dryden and W. Golden (eds), *Cognitive-Behavioural Approaches to Psychotherapy*. London: Harper & Row.

Wells, A. (1997) *Cognitive Therapy of Anxiety Disorders*. Chichester: Wiley.

Wessler, R. L. (1986) 'Conceptualizing cognitions in the cognitive-behavioural therapies', in W. Dryden and W. Golden (eds), *Cognitive-Behavioural Approaches to Psychotherapy*. London: Harper & Row.

White, C. A. (2001) *Cognitive Behaviour Therapy for Chronic Medical Problems*. Chichester: Wiley.

Wills, F. and Sanders, D. (1997) *Cognitive Therapy: Transforming the Image*. London: Sage Publications.

Wright, J. H., Thase, M. E., Beck, A. T. and Ludgate, J. W. (1993) *Cognitive Therapy with Inpatients*. New York: Guilford.

Young, J. E. (1994) *Cognitive Therapy for Personality Disorders: A Schema Focused Approach*, 2nd edn. Sarasota, Fla.: Professional Resource Press.

Young, J. E. (2002) 'Schema-focused therapy for personality disorders', in G. Simos (ed.), *Cognitive Behaviour Therapy: A Guide for the Practising Clinician*. Hove: Brunner-Routledge.

Young, J., Klosko, J. and Weisharr, M. (2003) *Schema Therapy: A Practitioner's Guide*. New York: Guilford.